SLOW TRAVELS IN UNSUNG SPAIN

BRETT HETHERINGTON

APOCRYPHILE
PRESS

THE APOCRYPHILE PRESS
Berkeley, CA
www.apocryphile.org

Copyright © 2019 by Brett Hetherington
All rights reserved.
ISBN 978-1-949643-04-6 | paperback
ISBN 978-1-949643-05-3 | epub

ALSO BY BRETT HETHERINGTON:

The Remade Parent (Nonfiction)

CONTENTS

CHAPTER 3—Córdoba—Page 74

"The Andalusian Wolfman"—Beer Wars—Sixto, Sitges and Barcelona's *Camp Nou*—'Tarshish:' legendary place of riches at the end of the world—into the Frying Pan of Andalucía—two Koreans —covered by a carpark: "one of the great cities of the Roman world"—Jesus' black tears—a most discreet casino and 'The Spanish Robin Hood'—"Take neither too much nor too little sun."

CHAPTER 4—*Interlude—Page 89*

As it is, as it was: Asturias—*Asturian coal miner: a portrait—The colours of Asturias: a poem*

CHAPTER 5—To Frigiliana—Page 95

Moseying not dithering—white hill towns: Aguilar de la Frontera, Monturque, Lucena—Truman Capote's spare shirt—Linda: a pilgrim's progress halted—A Shropshire lad in the 'sierras':—the wandering funeral—Virgil's fennel—nightmare in Nerja.

CHAPTER 6—In Jaen—Page 107

Where the dogs roam free—graffiti battles—liquid treasure— the mystery of the tram that wasn't—Arab Baths—no Hard Rock Cafe—Flamenco: a declaration, a pre-industrial human howl—a homeless couple—Tarbut Sefarad: Rafael—'miracle' on *Maestra* street—bumping into Judaism—cheesed off in 'The Little Fishes'—the town at night redeemed.

CHAPTER 7—In Ubeda—Page 122

The disappearing captain—Aunt Caterina—a certain house on a certain street: Antonio Muñoz Molina and the meaning of a chickpea—the hint of a Rambla—Synagogue of Water

CHAPTER 8—To Home—Page 131

Early Sunday morning: thirty teenagers on a train—"a self-banished Spaniard: Juan Goytisolo"—*preguntita-ed* again —a young man and his beard—"so sad I will never live here in Barcelona"—"don't go to *La Mina*"—the mean streets—'books by the metre:'—Lucia Graves—the King's Mills—Fungilab, Topcon, Rammer—The Devil's Bridge and Chupa Chups—Catalan nationalism: Josep —return to the grape.

TO ZARAGOZA

Today I was leaving my familiar little home patch to explore a much wider home. I took myself to our local train station and instead of heading into Barcelona city, as I usually did, this time I made sure to remember to go to the other side of the platform and get on a train going south—the way out of Catalonia. In my head was the idea to follow up on a desire to travel further into Spain's heated-up summer interior, especially to parts of it that I had not yet experienced and to places that were off the standard tourist trail.

In short, I had the appetite to see more of the country I had come to call home but this time bear witness with a different sensibility. I wanted to be a solo traveller again and find that other Spain, that *elsewhere*. I was hungry for the largeness of Spain, the expanse of it, but I had a destination in mind. Almost nine hundred kilometres away, I imagined the town called Ubeda as old, dusty, white and dry, and I planned it to be my turning circle, after which I would head home.

Ubeda was somewhere I had never been before. It is the hometown of Antonio Muñoz Molina, a Spanish writer I greatly admire. Amongst other desires, I had a question about him that I wanted to try to get an answer for. Could I recognise if the town of his upbringing had affected his novels? For many years, he had lived with his wife (also an accomplished writer) in both Madrid and New York, but as a young man he couldn't wait to get away from small-town Spain as quickly as possible.

I had a theory though that despite everything else in life, our childhood places make a mark on us all. Hesitating to think of this trip as a pilgrimage, for the moment I accepted that it may well look like it. As well as that, I had that fundamental buzz of excitement in the stomach that travel brings. And I was harbouring a wider and less specific urge; the very same one I had felt for the first time twenty years before: I wanted to find and live *the great night of Europe.*

At this rural train stop the sharp sun told me it was mid-morning. Usually near-deserted, before I lived near it this station had seemed to be in the middle of nowhere in particular. Over the previous couple of years it had become my routine to stand and wait for a train to the Catalan capital while looking across the vineyards to Montserrat's rock mountains, abruptly placed in the near distance. On clear days like today this range was like a well-painted backdrop to a stage set. On other days it gave the impression of a series of nature's gothic cathedrals clumped together. Montserrat: with its pre-Renaissance Benedictine monastery that Nazi SS leader Heinrich Himmler visited during World War II, bizarrely expecting to find the Holy Grail there for him to steal away.

Standing here alone, I typically also saw it as a kind of personal victory that no one was calling me on my mobile, bothering me. I breathed a sense of liberation from being released out of the decade-long bondage of being in a classroom with teenagers all day. I'd moved on to earning a wage by zipping around the edges of Barcelona city teaching adults English in different company offices and that was fine with me.

The train I was waiting for turned out to be twenty minutes late. But today it was not only the direction I was travelling in that was different. Stepping through the carriage doors, the first thing I heard was a young man singing. Probably Moroccan and with headphones on, he was making a throaty Arabic wail, which he soon mixed with Spanish words, completely indifferent to any other passenger's wishes for a quiet time.

Across from him, behind me, was an older man talking loudly in what seemed to be a drunken voice. He was telling a woman reading a book near me how pretty she was, slurring "...*Que linda...*" but he was still wearing sunglasses and this made him look insincere. She smiled shyly and when he got off the train fifteen minutes later he put on a baseball cap backwards. I saw he was wearing baggy trousers with his underpants showing—what one American writer calls "the uniform of the defeated." I wondered if this man knew that having his pants as low as this was originally a signal of sexual availability in prison.

At the medium-sized town of Vilafranca del Penedès a crowd got on the train, seemingly heading for the final stop on this line that curves back over a dozen kilometres to the beach. It was the last day of July. Eight years ago, to the day, along with my wife and our then-five year old son we had arrived in this town (which we had never seen before) to try living here. We had taken a week to drive through France and across the central Pyrenees mountains into Spain from our previous home in England. We'd made a good life here since then, though it was certainly not always an easy life.

The train rolled through the ever-present orderly lines of the vineyards of this region. The Phocians, an ancient Greek people (not to be confused with the Phoenicians), were the first to cultivate grapes in these fields in the fourth century BC. I looked back and gave a mental wave to the apartment block on the very edge of the town where we spent the first half of our time living here.

That memory made me think that surely, almost every time we travel there is an element of escape. In my case, I was glad to be getting away from some of the routines of domestic life. As comforting and familiar as repetition can be, and as much as I knew I'd be happy to eventually get home (just as I always did after

3

being absent) I felt a touch of guilt at leaving my wife with our son. Recently he had seemed intent on getting all his teenage bile out of himself in one foul burst before the age of fourteen.

The day before I left we'd just finally relented after a long period of resistance and allowed him to use his birthday money from his grandfather to buy an iPod. I just couldn't understand why he had gotten angry when we refused to give him our credit card details to pay online for some damn game. Peace and quiet had been avoiding me for what seemed like months. But sitting in my seat on this train, my mood was relaxed. In fact, my physical preparations for this trip had been minimal: packing cotton clothes, sunscreen and a couple of good books to read. Readying myself psychologically though had been extensive started months before.

Firstly, I reread Margaret Sayers Peden's clean and crisp English translation of Muñoz Molina's masterpiece of a novel titled "Sepharad." I had already read it once on a rare visit to Australia a couple of years before. Then, the book had given me an escape from a heavy sadness of the house we stayed in. I engrossed myself in it every night, lying with my wife Paula in her mother's bed in Canberra—while just ten metres away in the lounge room her eighty-five-year old mother, now with a jaundiced yellow-brown face, was flat out and unmoving on a special adjustable bed. She was slowly dying of cancer, hallucinating, eating very little and barely speaking. This for four months, with Paula as her main carer.

In Muñoz Molina's sweeping novel he had both invented the leading Jewish characters as well as taking them from real life, including authors Franz Kafka and the Italian genius Primo Levi. By the end of the book, his writing had left musical embers in me. I clearly knew his voice: (soft but clear) and when I heard him interviewed on a podcast months later he sounded confident, thoughtful and gentle; very much like I had expected.

Back home in Spain, I looked up possible train routes to get to Muñoz Molina's hometown in the inner south of the country and I studied maps of where I was thinking of going. Just like one of his frustrated males in the novel, "in the midst of such a low-key life, the (mere thought of) the trip was an almost physical pleasure, a sensation of ... lightness, as if leaving the station would free me from the habits and obligations that weighed me down."

From a piece of truth that I scarcely wished to fully admit, I had another motivation that had acutely sharpened my will. Like my mother and her mother before her, both of my kidneys were slowly failing: crammed with cysts and stones put there by a malevolent inherited trait. I had come to realise that if I didn't make this trip soon while I had the benefit of still-decent health, I may never get the chance to do something as strenuous again; at least until I had a transplanted organ.

Opposite me now on the train was an older man with a prominent bottom lip that jutted out. On his face he had a confused expression and he was looking at a mobile phone. As if to illustrate a worldwide generational difference, a few metres away a group of young girls were looking into the hand of the loudest one, peering at a little screen, pointing and laughing. Above them was an advertising sign for one of the Barcelona tourist buses. It pictured a few of the usual tourist sites in the city, featuring Gaudí's giant, still unfinished *Sagrada Familia* church and had the word "Puja!" in large text, meaning: climb, or in this context "Get On!" The train stopped at El Monjos ("the monks") and then slipped past twenty massive wine silos and the equally huge concrete factory that dominates the village. Local people here had for years been complaining about the pollution it created. A few short kilometres back down the line and through the stripes of vines in Vilafranca, where we used to live, on some windy days I would catch a whiff of what smelt to me like burnt cheese—a pong emitted by the concrete factory. Today, I poked my head out of the train door but there was no strong odour.

After the next stop at the town of L'Arboç were large olive plantations. This was a sign that the wine growing region around had once been eclipsed by more Arab traditions, though for a long time this was no man's land: a border between the Christian and Moorish kingdoms. I'd driven through the town's main street dozens of times and always got the feeling that I half-recognised something there that I couldn't put my finger on.

What I later learnt that I partly remembered was the sight of a half-scale replica of Seville's very photogenic Giralda minaret tower. The local myth was that it was built by a married couple homesick for Seville but in truth it was simply a homage to a memory, pointing skywards in this Catalan town, so far from Andalucía. Out of the train window I glimpsed the occasional '*masia*' (large country house) and running parallel with the line again were the blue lines of the AVE high-speed rail which I guessed I might be on when I came home later in the month.

Soon though I was surprised to be almost alone in the long carriage. El Vendrell—hometown of Pau Casals, the great cellist, conductor and Catalan political exile—had passed by, but not before my eye picked out the Magic America Sex Shop on the edge of town beside the railway line. Along with everybody else who was left, I got off at the final junction, Sant Vicenç de Calders, where a different line runs along the Garraf coast and then through Barcelona. At the ticket office I discovered that my next train inland was a few hours away.

Outside, near the station car park there was a sign that interested me. It said that this little corner of the country had been a strategic communications connection and that the brick station and surrounds were bombed and wrecked during the Spanish Civil War. Mussolini's Italian air force and German seaplanes were responsible for eighty-three deaths as well as injuring at least two hundred people from early 1938 until January the following year. In Mediterranean Europe, wherever you go, the past is close behind you.

In this part of Europe, 'the Med'—that often glorified five-million-year-old liquid highway, the world's largest inland sea—is also close. There was a holiday feel to the streets a few minutes' walk from the station. Groups of young girls were wearing that virtual summer uniform of cut-off jeans hot pants, in the style that some in the Catholic church were still publicly objecting to. Middle-aged couples in swimsuits struggled along with that particular heaviness that people can get when they are near a beach but not on it. I walked past restaurants with Russian language menus posted up and noted the Distress Jazz Club (not "de-stress" as they surely intended to call it).

Some of the visitors here today may well have been the same ones who had threatened to have their holidays away from this part of the coast. In the local media, a few Spaniards had made the absurd claim that the displays of the Catalan Flag (at least the version with the independence star on it) around the beach zone of Coma Ruga, were a "symbol of confrontation" to them and they had complained to the town council. Today would be the last I would see of the ocean for at least several weeks and that was exactly how I wanted it to be. I'd long had a theory that it was impossible to have an intelligent conversation on a beach and I was happy to leave it and the petty politics behind for an extended period of time. Catalonia was in the throes of trying to establish whether to continue as a part of wider Spain, or if not, how it would somehow gain its independence after a kind of referendum in the autumn. The possible breaking up of the Spanish 'union' was closer now than it had been for a long, long time.

But these concerns were the furthest thing from my mind. I had a train to catch but was getting a taste of that waiting time that travellers know so well, time to kill or fill, and like a particular strata of traveller, I was thinking that on my first day out and about I should conserve funds. To the sounds of a Romanian accordion player I sat with a beer for company and looked across the sand, ocean and horizon. As usual, I could never look at waves or surf for more than a couple of minutes. There was a very, very long pier on the northern side of the beach and it struck me that in all the years I'd lived here I'd seen very few of these structures at the Spanish or Catalan seaside.

Maybe I just hadn't been looking, though. Being in a place

outside of the usual can, at its best, have a sharpening of all the senses. As Alain de Boton found while philosophising in *The Art of Travel*, our state of mind is one of the most crucial factors when we get on a bus, a plane or even just go for a walk in our own home-towns. He suggests that with the right attitude we can find a fresh-ness and new stimulation from the all-too-familiar locations we take for granted every day.

Now though, it was two o'clock and people were starting to leave the beach. This *was* something I had noticed many times before—the entrenched custom of local people was to get out of the summer heat and go to lunch at this time of the day. Those who stay sunning themselves after that hour are almost entirely foreigners.

Across the road near the beach showers I watched a mother telling off her son in front of what seemed to be a large group of relatives. At first I couldn't hear her words, which turned what she was doing into a something like a silent movie pantomime. She was using some of the range of gestures that are characteristic of not just Iberian folk, but of Mediterraneans in general: the prayer hands turned inward to the body, the open palm indicating a griev-ance that no one could see and the pinching of the air, as if trying to grasp the essence of her point and trap it in her tanned fingers.

What was also interesting to me in the few moments when I could hear her were the pauses and the 'rhythm' of this woman's diatribe. (Rhythm being a very popular word across the country and in many different and surprising contexts.) She would break off from her ranting to chat with a member of the group for a few minutes, then turn back to her young victim and restart her task of castigating him. She did this several times, but after twenty minutes of standing around going nowhere, she eventually gave her son a few playful and forgiving slaps on the back and everyone went away together smiling, at peace. Here was a mini-episode that illustrated something I had also seen before in different situa-tions. It was the Spanish habit of taking something unpleasant, wringing the emotion out of it, then going back to the good-heartedness that is such a marked part of life lived in public here. Even a severe scolding can end enjoyably.

At the station I waited for my regional train that would take me almost directly west to Zaragoza, the modern day regional capital of what had once been the medieval Kingdom of Aragon. Other different lines from here on the coast could have taken me through the biblical sounding Salomó and across to Lleida or along the coast through the tourist resort of Salou, onto riverside Tortosa then, after oceans of orange groves, a final stop at the large port city of Valencia.

Today was the first of two days of industrial action on all the lines across the country that were run by the organisation known as RENFE. I knew that there was a reduced timetable operating because the CCCO (the same trade union that I was also a member of) had been protesting against, among other things, a decision to axe the number of staff who dealt with the public. In the waiting room I asked a man in a white singlet vest if he knew why the workers were striking.

"We always have to pay and pay," he grunted, chewing on a toothpick, ignoring my question. "It's us, the average person, who gets the sharp end of the stick. And politicians, *Ay!* From both the left and the right. And now Jordi Pujol. What a mountain of lies!"

Jordi Pujol was an ex-Catalan leader and still a hero to many in Catalonia. In the early 1960s he had been jailed for two years under the Franco dictatorship and had later been elected as President of Catalonia's government, holding the position for more than twenty years. He was now in the spotlight again as the latest in a long, grey line of seemingly never-ending corruption cases involving figures from all the major political parties. One estimate is that a total of six billion euros of public money disappeared in a single fifteen-year period.

Pujol had recently admitted that over more than three decades he hid a personal fortune in secret foreign bank accounts. The newest revelations included two of his seven children (also politicians) who were being investigated by judges for corruption and "influence-trafficking." This summer, his haggard face and corpulent body scuttling away from the media was to be a regular sight on the TV news.

Pujol was gradually being drowned in a whirlpool of lies and deceit, but later in the year, even as the details of his criminal actions came more clearly into the light, there was still an attitude towards him that bewildered me. Two Catalan men that I know quite well, one retired and the other a young banker, wanted to wait to see if Pujol would actually be proven to have broken the law before forming any opinion against him.

Both men knew that it would take a very long time for all the murky details to be thrashed out in court and that Pujol could even have died by the time the sloth-paced Spanish justice system came to a verdict. My banker acquaintance even giggled when he reluctantly acknowledged that Pujol had in fact admitted to stashing those millions of euros in a Swiss bank account. He offered the theory that Pujol had made these funds from business or inherited them from his father, who had been a hugely successful foreign exchange broker in the Franco years at a time when it was technically illegal to sell Spanish currency, though the practice was 'tolerated' by the authorities. I suggested that this was allowed because the 'tolerators' were paid off. "Of course!" my young friend agreed.

Out on the platform at the tail end of a long wait, a man sitting on the concrete asked me where I was from. "Ah, Cricket!" he exclaimed, when I told him I was originally from Australia. His name was Ahmed and like me, he hailed from a capital city—in his case, Islamabad, Pakistan. In Spain, he'd lived and worked in Logroño in the Rioja area as well as in the nearby town of Reus, where he was now living with his wife and three kids. Ahmed told me his job was behind the counter at one of the chain supermarkets called 'Día el Día.' Some of these kinds of convenience minimarts were owned and run by immigrants, especially Pakistanis. In Barcelona another common occupation for Pakistanis is barbers. But they don't just cut hair. The standard extra service that many do involves having your nose hair and ear hair clipped, whether you ask for it or not. I told Ahmed that I planned to go to Extremadura next week, but he hadn't heard of that place.

"Australia is a better country," he stated. "In Pakistan we have the Taliban. They are crazy. They get onto buses and trains and just shoot anyone they see."

We got on without any bloodshed when our train came. But five minutes into the trip, mild level violence was a distinct possibility. Sitting directly behind me were a young boy and girl who continued to kick my seat. I could tell they were brother and sister by the way they set up a repetitive pattern of needling each other. The boy told their grandmother he wanted to go to the beach *today* but his sister kept stirring him by saying they'd be going tomorrow instead.

"Hoy."

"Mañana."

"Hoy."

"Mañana."

"Hoy."

"Mañana."

"Hoy."

"Mañana."

"Shut up," the grandmother said quietly.

"Hoy."

"Mañana."

"Hoy."

"Mañana."

"Hoy."

"Mañana."

"Hoy."

"Mañana."

This verbal tennis went on for a full five minutes. It was loud enough to be difficult to ignore but, as was standard for this country, the other passengers just half looked on with indulgent smiles. Not a word of complaint was uttered, although some of them were clearly watching this little Abbott and Costello routine more closely.

"Hoy."

"Mañana."

"Hoy."

"Mañana."

"Hoy."

"Mañana."

"Hoy."

SLAP!

It seemed like the grandmother had reached the limit of her patience. But I could hear her laughing as she hit one of them. She had struck out while barely interrupting her conversation with a person across the aisle from her. The kid began to cry.

This could be the kind of drudgery that might lead you to think twice about travelling in Europe in August. But because it was Spain, the atmosphere was not tense. My thoughts of saying something to the kids did not last and the grandmother's handiwork was more of a surprise for her grandson than a blow that physically hurt him. To me, though, it was a lazy and contemptible act.

In fact, the truth is that Spain would virtually fall apart without the *abuela*: women like this grandmother. They are a one-woman national child care institution that has allowed the last few generations of mothers to do paid work away from home while *abuelita* looks after the little ones before school, after school and especially on holidays, including the three-month summer marathon break. Grandparents are vital to the Spanish family unit in a variety of ways, but especially because organised child care is appallingly fragmented and available unevenly. It can be relatively cheap and often has good activities for the children, but there are fewer and fewer government subsidised places, particularly since "the crisis" started, along with public sector budget slashing in 2008 and every year after that.

And these often dominating matriarchs and bastions of society seem to sense their own huge importance. They are generally the worst at pushing into queues in shops, often interjecting with "*Una preguntita...*" meaning "I just have a little question." Or they will pretend to not even notice a line of people waiting for service in a bank, for example. In many senses, they come from another era in Spain, from a time when the greatest thing a woman could do was produce babies, and the more babies you produced the more status you produced. In the forty-five years of General Franco's dictatorship, fertility was almost as virtuous as nobility.

Once, my family and I were given a tour through a lovely old cave-like house by an older man who was still a Franco supporter. He boasted and showed off objects in his home. But his proudest possession was a large black and white photo of his family of fifteen children.

Also long-established in Spain is the practice where both the mother and mother-in-law have the well accepted right to constantly meddle in the affairs of their own grown-up children, especially when it comes to child raising. I know a number of newer mothers who talk about moving cities or countries just to get away from the carping voices of their own mother or that of their partner. Precious few do actually make the move away, though. The bonds are inevitably too strong.

So, like a young mum obeying her elder's dietary directives, this train with its cargo of grandmothers, infants, immigrants and others followed the guidance of the coast. For the cost of a ticket it gave long, wide views out across the Mediterranean Sea, the same "big salt lake" that controversial French writer Jean Genet reportedly said "wanted to make him crap." On a wall between the train and the sea in large graffitied Catalan were words meaning "We will decide."

A pseudo-referendum on Catalan independence was coming, but I was going. So were about a dozen Africans. All young males, they got off carrying large bundles. These men were some of the so-called '*top mantas*:' street-sellers mainly from countries such as Senegal, Guinea-Bissau, Sierra Leone and Ghana. They had to always be on the watch for police as it is technically illegal to make a living by wandering through the crowds on beaches, hawking fake designer bags, sunglasses, hats, or selling pirated DVDs off a blanket (*manta*) on the ground. The standard penalty was a five hundred euro fine.

At the beach where I like to go with my family (just further back up the coast at Playa Sant Salvador) I had seen a campaign against these men spray painted on the pavements. These and other protests against them were largely run by local business people looking for a scapegoat to blame for a drop in sales. In some media reports they had made the nonsensical claim that the *top mantas* were the single biggest reason for a number of smaller shops having to close down. At two major spots at nearby El Vendrell and Calafell, a progressive experiment in confining them to particular zones had been tried three years previously. Unfortunately, it was scrapped after a supposed "storm of complaints from local entrepreneurs and tourism professionals" and the police crackdowns then extended to even fining members of the public for buying goods from *top mantas* at some seaside locations in Catalonia, including Barcelona.

But I was content to be leaving the coast behind—all the modern day fracking and nuclear plants of Tarragona, which historian Hilaire Belloc in 1920 had called that "dignified...most orderly, most compact" of Spain's Roman cities. I ignored all the commercial 'adventure parks' crammed with mainly British and German package tourists at Salou ("Visit us!" said yet another simplistic slogan) and we veered away from the chemical industries that regularly offend the eyes along this eastern stretch of coast.

A century and a half ago Welshman Robert Napper, one of Europe's pioneers of documentary photography, had spent time here taking shots of the poor and the land they struggled to live in. He had most likely been on this train line. It bends inland and stops at the aptly named '*Vila Seca*' (Dry Town.) Passing through olive groves on both the left and right, which at times enclosed the train in a roofless tunnel, this passenger carrier was then gently ringed in by distant mountains on three sides.

Next, we arrived at Reus, a kind of Muslim capital of Catalonia where there are those particular strains of social tensions that can come about with large numbers of immigrants who appear to be noticeable. The majority of Muslims living here are actually ethnic Berbers from the Rif in Morocco, many with their own Berber tribal language, full of the sound of hissing S's. I wished Ahmed a 'Ma al-salāmah' goodbye as he got off, forgetting that his first language was not Arabic or Berber, but Urdu. Reus, where he lives, is in fact a big enough town to have an airport with flights to foreign destinations. EasyJet regularly flies to the UK, for example, from this base, one that looks like a former military hangar.

Next to the station platform were two Spanish government advertising signs. One said: "Spain, you carry your destiny inside you," and the other proclaimed: "Go on holiday to the country that you know without knowing it." Slightly confusing to me, at least that was more imaginative than the usual RENFE ads *inside* the carriages.

If I'd been on this train in the same month but back in 1992—the year of the Barcelona Olympics—I might have seen something quite remarkable. A young man named Andreu Mateu had roller-skated through the town, returning to his birthplace of this town of Reus. He had propelled himself all the way there (a mere 120 kilometres) on inline skates, having started from the top of Barcelona's Tibidabo, a landmark mountain. In fact, this was just one of the 130 methods of transportation he used in his three-year trip through 120 countries, which he documented in his book, *Transcovery*. Mateu later went on to be the first Spaniard to row solo across the Atlantic as well swim across the Straits of Gibraltar and traverse the entire length of Africa by motorbike.

I had made the assumption that the sea was now well behind, but before the station at Riu de Canyes (Cane River) the rocky mountains and high church-towers allowed a view back towards the Med; a blue patch and Tarragona a beige smear: the colour was a sign of pollution. Petrochemical industries were being reported as a major cause of more than half of the region's men having 'poor quality' sperm—possibly the worst in the country, according to one local newspaper.

By the side of the tracks I saw large wild cactuses massed together, then a bit of graffiti that said "Fuck RENFE!" I supposed that some travellers would have wholeheartedly agreed with this sentiment because of the train strike known as a '*vaga*.' In Catalan 'vaga' means to strike but it also suggests other overtones because in Castilian Spanish the word can mean lazy, or to wander or roam around like a vagabond.

Unlike some, who might have been delayed longer than me, I was a fairly happy chappy, though. The still warm evening sun was slanting onto one side of my face and this train was going slow enough to pick out details in the landscape—deep ravines of pines, slanting terraces of olive plantations and modern wind turbines lining the sharp tips of the Serra de Llaberia Mountains further off. The air conditioning was ridiculously cold but the seats were comfortable.

The train stopped suddenly. Before long, a RENFE employee —it could only have been the driver himself—moved quickly through the carriage. It took a passenger to tell him which emergency brake a "boy" had flicked on as some kind of joke.

Looking out the window at the grapevines, scrubby bushes and sandy soil, I started to get the sense that I was almost out of Catalonia. (Later, I checked the map and found out that I was close to being right. The border with Aragon province was less than thirty kilometres away.) This area was the *Priorat*—a fact confirmed by the words "Skinheads Priorat" scrawled across one of the station's walls. I suspected that the local neo-Nazis would have had no idea that the Segre River that runs north near here towards the city of Lleida once gave its name to some local people. Five hundred years ago the ancestors of Auschwitz survivor and author Primo Levi took their family name from it before they left for southern France, then finally Turin.

In between a series of long tunnels I was reading an autobiography by Juan Goytisolo. Born in Barcelona, as a child he had lost his mother to the first of General Franco's many bombings of the city during the Civil War of the mid-1930s. She had been crushed and buried under the rubble of a collapsed building near Passeig de Gracia, one of Barcelona's major shopping avenues. Eventually, Goytisolo moved to France and later to Marrakesh, where he still lives today. Six months after my travels he would be given the Cervantes Prize, which Spain's Culture Ministry awards annually to recognise the life's work of a Spanish-language writer. This book (or at least the brilliant English translation of it by Peter Bush) titled *Forbidden Territory and Realms of Strife* was to be my company and sometimes a source of a consolation during moments of solitude over the coming weeks.

As an author I liked Goytisolo because of his clear and direct prose but I was also finding him to be a kindred spirit. Like me, he feels more at home away from the middle-class surroundings of his childhood, being captivated too by Paris, Marrakech, New York and Istanbul. We also shared a 'seminal' love of the desert, he living near it, as well as writing about Spain's Almeria desert towns in his travelogue, *Campos de Níjar*.

After reading a few pages of his autobiography I dozed off and woke up soon to the surprising and contrasting sight of water skiers on what looked like a wide canal. Its banks seemed manmade to me, but in fact, this was a spot called *Riba-roja*, just a narrow part of the long, long Ebro River (Spain's biggest in volume) that starts in the north of the country in Cantabria before working its way through the mountains and down to the Mediterranean in the south of Catalonia. Fish from the Ebro have been found to be excessively high in mercury and the European Union has prohibited their sale. Large tuna, swordfish and shark from the Med are also often notably high in mercury, but have not yet been banned by the EU.

The sight of all this dark, shiny water was stunning to my sleepy eyes because the land before it had been so parched. When

I'd looked into the rugged and stony land I thought of rabbits, but here were people sitting having barbeques next to this river that coursed parallel with the train track for the next few kilometres. We passed across more chalky ground, desolate and stratified. Abandoned, roofless brick buildings faced up into the sky and only the occasional pig shed stood complete. This was how Goytisolo too had witnessed it: "...*the exhausted tranquility of mountains of tight rumps,...(an) orphaned landscape,...an almost African land.*"

Along this stretch the Ebro became the snaking form of the *Embalse de Mequinenza*, an area popular for illegal fishing. Next was Nonaspe: a town that perched like a multi-backed bird clinging to the hill line. There were only two cars in its station car park.

And now we were in Aragon province.

Outside, at least according to the train temperature monitor, it was still 38 degrees, though the time was 7.30 pm. At a station named Fabara no town could be seen at all. But even here, in what otherwise appeared to be an isolated area, I could see that the rubbly land was being cultivated. Little stone huts and tyre tracks showed that farmers or maybe partridge hunters had recently visited here. These quiet, almost empty places were important to someone. The land gave up its bounty, just as it had for century after century. Apart from the deep forests of the north and west of Spain, almost inevitably in this country, some evidence of humanity, of a man-made structure could be seen, no matter where you were. Until the latter half of the 20th century Spain had long been made up of peasants, farmers, and wanderers, and these kinds of lives had continued in dwindling numbers despite the sad existence of remote rural-parts villages, where everyone had left and gone for good to the bigger towns and cities.

It had now gone up to 39 degrees. The train pushed on, a ripple of dark mountains on one side. As I looked off to the highway, I glimpsed the first vehicle I'd seen in an hour or so: a truck carrying bales of hay towards what looked like a salt lake.

"*No, un tractor,*" I heard someone say near me, as if they had known what I was thinking. A young bearded man was excitedly bringing what must have been his girlfriend over to my side of the train to show her something through the window.

"My mother's place," he said in Spanish, pointing off to the horizon.

But I could see absolutely nothing and the girlfriend did not react either. Just like many hundreds of thousands of Spaniards, he was going back to the *pueblo*, the town where he or his parents had grown up. For millions of his compatriots this too was one of the expected national customs of August. The young couple were the only ones who got off at the tiny station of Samper de Calanda, where low, dome-like rounded hills crowned the distance.

In my notebook I wrote that the next twenty minutes or so were "uneventful." I put this down to the monotonous sights of those industrial zones that ring most Spanish towns: Zaragoza being no exception. What I didn't know, as I sat staring out the window—now impatient to arrive—was that across the other side of the train track was an area of steppe called Los Monegros. On horseback through here, on their way to Barcelona, Miguel de Cervantes' fictional (now 400-year old) knight Don Quixote and his 'squire' Sancho also found that "over six days nothing happened to them worthy of putting in writing." That made me smile when I read it in a newspaper a few months later on.

Quixote, certainly Spanish literature's most famous character, apparently avoided Zaragoza, though it's not clear why. Almost all specialists in Cervantes work have been said to agree that Quixote and his squire crossed the Ebro River outside of the city, where it would be possible in the summer when droughts lower the water flow.

In another invented bit of the unlikely culture around this area, Bigas Luna's film *Jamón, Jamón* filmed scenes with his protagonists at the toll station near a small town called El Ciervo (The Crow). The movie meant a lot to me when I first saw it in the mid-1990s. Its landscapes and equally raw erotic qualities were one of the factors that made me want to visit Spain. Perhaps unsurprisingly, according to one local man reported in the national press, "here there are no tourists."

Only half an hour's drive up the country from this unlikely spot, small numbers of visitors were starting to come for reasons of history though. In the winter of 1937, George Orwell, one of my literary heroes and somewhat of a quixotic individual himself, fought about twenty kilometres northeast of Zaragoza around Alcubierre—a town that reminded one 21st century Orwell pilgrim of "a small market town in Ireland, though a lot drier and hotter of course" than nearby Huesca. Orwell was a member of the International Brigades in the Civil War against Franco, but wrote in *Homage to Catalonia* that his greatest enemy was the severe cold and the dreary inactivity of trench warfare before he caught a bullet in the neck and ended up convalescing in strife-torn Barcelona.

Very nearby, to the south is another site that the Civil War had made significant. Mortar shells and gunfire turned the village of Belchite into an abandoned ghost town. According to historian Cecil D. Eby, in 1937, in the middle of the conflict, "*(journalists, who included Ernest Hemingway) found a town so totally ruined that often one could not tell where the streets had been. People were digging under piles of mortar, bricks, and beams pulling out corpses. Mule carcasses, cooking pots, framed lithographs, sewing machines—all covered with flies—made a surreal collage. Belchite was less a town than a nasty smell.*"

Alluring to visitors in a macabre way because of the hideous devastation that it is still there to be clearly seen, I would never have stopped at Belchite. It has become a major meeting point for General Franco's sympathisers, who still hold onto his memory with a sick fervour. The dictator himself had ordered that the old town be left as a shell in its bombed-out state—this as a message to his enemies—and in a further statement of his power, a new town was built overlooking the old one. Apparently, the new Belchite was built by captured Republican soldiers who were thrown in the nearby concentration camp that carried the village name.

❦

ZARAGOZA PORTILLO STATION WAS SURPRISINGLY QUIET INSIDE. I was one of only a handful of passengers to step off the train, but then again it was the middle of summer. Almost as soon as I'd arrived and checked into my hotel, with the calling freedom of the twilight I headed to the nearest tapas bar. Immediately I noticed some distinct differences compared to Catalan tapas. There was a clear preference for small quail eggs as a topping for meat or sausage when placed on its customary small round of bread. Also, elsewhere in Spain I'd never remembered noticing large gherkins used to take a stuffing of tuna and draped with a single anchovy. Here there were plenty on offer.

The next day the food oddity continued. In the massive, century-old municipal food market sitting beside the new tram line I found a type of mini-swordfish called *auja* that I had never seen before. There was also an odd-looking cheese—a *tronchon* sheep cheese made by the *Sardon* Company, something that could have easily been mistaken for a British pork pie. At another seafood stall for thirty-nine euros a kilo they were selling *percebes*— a gooseneck barnacle crustacean that northern Galicians risk their own necks for in the process of scraping them off the steep, slippery rocks in the often fierce Atlantic Ocean.

In this market I also detected an element of regional rivalry. The national sausage of Catalonia is the *botifarra,* but here it was being labelled as the 'butifarra of Aragon.' Likewise, the ribbed tomato called a 'Montserrat' in Catalonia was rebranded as a 'Tomato of Aragon.' I'd been told by some Catalans that a few of their friends had been insulted in the streets of Aragon when they spoke their own language, but maybe I shouldn't have been surprised to find the politics of Spanish history also played out in the arena of gastronomy.

Another thing that was even more astounding was the sheer expanse of this "central" market itself. It was crowded with shoppers and I lost count of the number of individual shops or stalls under this one huge roof. I asked around and found an information board which gave the names of an astonishing twenty-three fruit and vegetable sellers, twenty-two butchers and twenty fish shops. A handful of these were specialists catering specifically to the South American, Chinese or even African communities, but all this for a city with a population of 682,000 gives an idea of how important food is to the average Spaniard.

Outside at the bottom of the steps of the market, I met someone who was not at all average and certainly not your average pauper. With one arm in a sling, a tall long-haired woman of about sixty approached me saying:

"Please, I need a kilo of tomatoes, a kilo of onions and a kilo of red and green peppers."

"I'm very sorry," I said and slowly moved away down the square towards some empty benches. I watched the woman continue to walk from person to person with her request of this trio of vegetables, but she was ignored by all of them. A few metres from where I sat there was a large statue of Caesar Augustus pointing off towards the river. I took this as a signal that the begging woman would have better luck going in the same direction he was indicating, but now she had approached me again.

"Please, I need a kilo of tomatoes, a kilo of onions and a kilo of red and green peppers," she repeated in the same flat, mournful tone as the first time. Her eyes were glassy.

"Why do you have no money?" I asked her quietly.

"I have had no help," she replied. "I have six children. I live in the other part of the city and it has been twenty days since I have had money. Please, I need a kilo of tomatoes, a kilo of onions and a kilo of red and green peppers."

I could hear in her voice that she was speaking on a kind of autopilot and her dark eyes were pleading. With my eye contact she must have sensed that I was softening and she slowly reached out and touched my cheek with a soft hand. In that moment my will was broken and I realised she had moved me.

"Okay," I said. "Just wait here a minute and I'll come back with what you are asking for."

I walked back into the market wondering why I had been persuaded by this woman and it struck me that her begging was not abstract. She'd practically given me a recipe for summer *gazpacho* soup and I imagined her singing while she cut up the ingredients in a cramped kitchen. When I brought the vegetables back to her she asked me pointedly what I had got. With a smile I told her and handed the full plastic bag to her. But this did not satisfy her and she asked me for bread too. I laughed at her audacity and walked away while she moved on to her next target.

A well-dressed older man with his own shopping bags of food had been watching and listening to my conversation. "Excuse me, but that woman you bought things for," he started, "she shouldn't be bothering people in that way. Why doesn't she go to the charity up the road and get her food there?" It was a rhetorical question. He continued, "She's here regularly, you know, and she doesn't need to be. She just comes here when she's hungry."

"Don't you think there must be a reason why she doesn't go to a charity?" I asked. "Maybe she's had a problem with them before or just doesn't like going there," I continued. "It would certainly be easier than having to spend so much time asking people to buy food for her, wouldn't it?"

"No," the man said firmly. He gestured for me to walk with him and together we casually ambled down towards the river. I suggested that the woman had a talent for what she was doing. I gave him my instinctive opinion: she wasn't really annoying people badly and could simply be ignored, just as most people did.

"But she pesters everybody," the man repeated.

"Yes, but at a charity she wouldn't get any fresh food, which is better for our health," I maintained. "Is this woman a gypsy?"

"No, she is not that kind of person," he replied with a slight shake of the head. His tram was arriving and he ran to catch it.

I thought again about the woman who I had bought the vegetables for. She was such a contrast to the more conventional beggars where I lived. Most commonly they sit or kneel, some with their heads fixed facing down. Usually they have a hand-written sign telling of how they have children but no work or are sick. Some are part of a well-organised Romanian group but many others are not.

For me as a child, I had never knowingly seen begging because the city where I'd grown up in is the prosperous, public-service based capital of Australia. Poverty was well hidden by being almost entirely confined to a few small suburban areas. Until I'd first trav-elled in Europe twenty years ago, as an adult I had not been exposed to anything like the street sleepers in Paris, who are made all the more moving by their canine companions looking better-fed than they are. Still remaining in my memory too is the sight of two middle-aged men on a bus in Naples. They made an announcement to the passengers, then rolled up their trousers and pointed to boils and abscesses on their legs as proof of their suffering.

Those kinds of scenes had produced a sensation that was new to me: a mix of sympathy or sadness as well as the desire to help contrasted with a feeling of frustrated impotence. At first I was fascinated but sometimes even repulsed, as I still can be. In my daily life in Catalonia I have almost become accustomed to being asked for money or food. I've developed a simple policy of almost never giving cash because there is no guarantee that it will be used for survival and may be used for drugs or alcohol. Occasionally, I offer to buy bread or other food for someone who appears to be needy and will regularly do this when asked.

American aristocrat author Tryphosa Bates-Batcheller observed in her trips across Spain just before the First World War that "even the beggars call you 'little brother or sister' when they ask for alms." I have not experienced that particular language but am obviously a sucker for the kind of methods used by the woman outside Zaragoza's municipal food market.

Parallel to the tramline where the anti-beggar man and I had walked to, the Ebro River looked decidedly less healthy than where I'd seen it just the day before outside the city. There was a powder pastel current on the surface moving slowly, and patches of sinister green moss were collecting with intent on its banks. Nearby I saw traffic on the *Puente de Santiago* bridge. It was here where, in a custom adopted from a bridge in Rome, romantic couples attach a padlock to the rails of the bridge. They write their names on the lock and throw the key into the river as a symbol of eternal love.

In front of the bridge I saw the characteristic "pilgrim's scallop shell" imprinted into the pavement by the roadside—the first indication I'd seen on this trip of the famous *Camino de Santiago*. Often thought to be originally a walking path for the devout to go to stare at the supposed bones of Saint James at the huge church in Santiago de Compostela over in Galicia (more than 800 kilometres west of Zaragoza), the truth is quite different.

Like so many pre-Christian activities, the Catholic Church had pragmatically adapted the *Camino*. At one time, pagans used to walk across northern Spain and end up at Fisterra (the symbolic end of the world) where they would ritually burn their clothes and then watch the sun drop slowly into the sea across *La Costa de la Muerte* (the Coast of Death.)

Here in Zaragoza, however, this bridge takes you only as far as the other side of the river. As an alternative, closer to the older part of town there is the now more pedestrian-friendly Old Stone One, *el Puente Piedra*. It is guarded by a statue of two lions with particularly prominent testicles. Just before the bridge I'd seen another piece of simplistic advertising for a local water park. "*Mojate!*" it exhorted. "Get (yourself) wet!

Next to a baroque-style church called *San Juan de los Panetes* (Saint John of the Bread Rolls) I came across a small memorial to victims of terrorism "against civilians and military personnel" that "occurred" there on the 30th of January 1987. What the plaque did not detail was that a (recently disbanded) Basque terrorist organisation was found to be responsible for the death of two people and the injuring of more than thirty-five on this day. As recently as October 3 of the previous year there had been a different incident at the nearby basilica of El Pilar, but this time the home-made bomb was defused by police. The suspects, from an anarchist group known as Insurrectional Commando Mateo Morral, were also reported to be responsible for a similar failed attempt to blow up Madrid's Almudena Cathedral in February of 2013.

A couple of streets away the religious theme continued at a shop that was obviously visited by some of the pilgrims on their way to a footsore glory. Displayed in the front window was all the usual tack: ugly and cheap charms, miniature virgin figurines and saintly types blessing families. One particular item caught my eye. For three euros customers could also invest in something called a LUCKY ANGEL KEY. I translated the accompanying instructions as, "the legend says that you should think of your seven wishes from the smallest to the greatest. When you turn the key to the right it closes the path of bad energy that comes into your life. Turning the key the other way opens the gates to luck, health and abundance."

Maybe naively, I was a bit stunned that this kind of absurd and deceptive product was still being sold (and presumably bought) in the 21st century, not in some crummy magazine or dodgy website, but in broad daylight in a shop on a main street of a major city. I went inside and asked the pretty young girl behind the counter how this key was supposed to work.

"You just put it around your neck. It's a necklace," she explained.

"Yes," I said, "but what would it do for me?"

"It brings luck."

"But how do the angels help me?" I asked.

"Nothing, it's just a necklace."

"You said it brings luck," I calmly insisted. "What is the actual process that occurs so that I am luckier?"

"Nothing, it's just a necklace," she repeated. "Women usually buy it when they want to get pregnant."

"Oh, I see." I hesitated. "And there are other things that are needed to get pregnant, aren't there?" I joked. "Do you believe it really helps women in that way?"

"No, no." The shop assistant looked away, smiling shyly. She turned and pretended that she had something else to do next to the counter.

"So, should I ask God and the angels for help too?" I continued.

"No, no, I don't think so."

"Then are you an atheist?" I prodded.

"Yes. Yes, I am."

"But you are selling these things called lucky angel keys for three euros and other religious things here," I countered. "Why?"

The young woman now started to go red in the face and her delicate smile became coyer.

"I can see you're a bit embarrassed. Don't worry. I'm an atheist too," I said smiling back. "It's okay, I'll go now. Thanks for your time."

Wandering across the road, I came into a massive square flanked with grand buildings. This turned out to be the 200-metre-long *Plaza Nuestra Señora del Pilar*—including the church built at the spot where the Virgin Mary supposedly appeared on a pillar (with those angels again) in front of James the Great, one of the original Jesus-buddy apostles back in AD 39 or the 2nd of January AD 40, depending on who you believe. At the time he was praying, or preaching, also depending on who you believe.

On one side of the huge open square there was a lovely statue of a horse. I watched some young children play on it, riding its back like pint-sized warriors in T-shirts. Before much longer an adult man also came and sat on the horse. He posed, doing an impression of a wacky Gangnam-style cowboy while his female partner took photo after photo. To me, this guy personified one of the main differences between a tourist and a traveller. A tourist certainly doesn't care enough to attempt to read the plaque on the statue's base and doesn't really even look at any details of the statue itself. A traveller with some curiosity may well do. The mentality of the tourist is that the world outside their home country is there as a kind of playground, a stage set for easy fun and laughs, with or without excess alcohol as a stimulant.

I found the office for tourists on the opposite side of this vast rectangular area that was now a piece of open geometry burning in the sun. It wasn't busy inside and from the promotional poster outside the building it wasn't difficult to work out why tourists were relatively small in number in this part of Spain. In the pictures chosen for display on the poster, this region of Aragon was being depicted with very much the same kind of advertising images as I'd seen for most other parts of the country: attractive, smiling young women in traditional costume at a fiesta/parade, excited children at the obligatory aquarium (in this case yelling into megaphones—loud noises are great fun!) and for the adults some white-water rafting and wine-tasting. This was all set against a landscape of modern buildings; why so, when the old ones were so alluring? Here, in its presentation to the public, the difference between this region and, say, one of the coastal resorts was almost impossible to discern.

And yet, Zaragoza has such a wealth of history and culture going for it, as I was quickly finding. Judging from the tourism agency's most prominent bit of work—and probably also its most expensive—the city and its region was just another place with the usual run-of-the-mill attractions, but without beaches.

Still, I was more than happy not to have a lot of competition for viewing space at the *Ibercaja* museum just around the corner. Sponsored by the bank of the same name, as part of its "social work," it featured an exhibition of Zaragoza's favourite son—Francisco Goya—mainly showing his (pre-1820s) nightmarish black and white *aguafuerte* and *aguatinta* etchings, though the word 'etchings' sounds much too tame for this collection.

The artist gives the gallery visitor a disturbing spectrum of his imagination: creeping, sinister figures with the gauntest of faces; double-headed and bare-breasted harpies; demented, dancing ghouls; vicious birds of prey; cringing victims of un-shown atrocities; fierce, frotting, winged creatures; hook-nosed, bug-eyed peasants; the limbless impaled on stakes; skeletons with over-sized muscles; otherwise ordinary-looking men with shocking, hollow eyes and squashed faces at prayer in obsequious postures while being taunted by hairless carnival clowns alongside sharp-toothed elves; baboon-humans farting flames and a donkey in a gentleman's finest clothes.

All of these were described in the museum as *"personajes que no son de este mundo"*—characters that are not of this world. Personally, I disagreed strongly with the official museum comment that this gallery showed "the most mysterious and enigmatic side" to Goya's art. I saw it all as his stark interpretation of human vanity and fear.

Another Australian had also looked at Goya's portrayals of war and felt compelled to write. In a typically insightful moment, Robert Hughes speculated that a European might not have reacted in quite the same way as he had because explicit war photographs were almost never published in Australia before the 1960s. One of that country's few truly great writers, with characteristic clarity and intensity, Hughes declared in his penetrating book on the artist:

"At fifteen, to find this voice (from Goya)—*so finely wrought and yet so raw, public and yet strangely private—speaking to me with such insistence and urgency from a remote time and a country I'd never been to, of whose language I spoke not a word, was no small thing. It had the feeling of a message transmitted with terrible urgency, mouth to ear: this is the truth, you must know this, I have been through it. Or, as Goya scratched at the bottom of his copper plates in* Los desastres de la guerra: *"Yo lo vi" "I saw it." "It" was unbelievably strange, but the "yo" made it believable."*

Goya's work had a similar effect on me in the quiet of this gallery. The collection had credibility - in every sense of the word —because it is often the nightmares and not the pleasant dreams that stay with us.

In another room of the museum, near a few of Goya's earlier royal portraits (that to my eyes seemed like ridiculous flattery) I happened to notice a pen and ink mountain scene with birds flying above the simple landscape. The German Nobel Prize winner for Literature Günter Grass had passed by this way just ten years earlier and this was one of his artistic efforts.

Soon after I sat down to a small lunch of fresh prawns at a small, empty restaurant on an equally small square. Through the window I noticed a poster that took up half a wall of the square. Alongside pictures of serious faces of both genders it said: "890 men work as nurses in Aragon. And you still think that this is women's work?" (Then below:) "154 women work as local police. And you still think this is men's work?"

As attested by the blue flag with a circle of stars, this attempt at informing society was sponsored by the Zaragoza town council but was funded by the European Union. It was the kind of publicly financed campaign, focusing on perceptions of human rights that in Catalonia barely existed, because there the government had prioritised money for telling the populace almost exclusively about the independence question and the referendum that was planned to take place in November. In fact, the front page of the local edition of *El Periodico* newspaper was reporting a meeting between Spanish Prime Minister Mariano Rajoy and the Catalan '*lider*' (i.e. leader) Artur Mas. The two men were shown smiling weakly, shaking hands and, rather aptly, looking in opposite directions. "La esperada reunión...concluyó ayer" were the words used, a translation being "The anticipated meeting concluded yesterday."

Having lived in this country for eight years, it occurred to me regularly that *esperada* also means 'hoped for,' as well as 'expected.'

The article stated that they "disagreed about the referendum (going ahead) but were dialoguing." It was only in a second smaller piece on page twenty of the paper that Mas was given his correct title of President. Two months later Prime Minister Rajoy was quoted as saying that a new "chapter of dialogue" was being opened with Catalonia after the highest Spanish Constitutional court had declared the planned referendum illegal. He also "threatened to block a non-binding 'consultation' ballot which Catalonia says it will hold instead."

So, there were cracks but somehow 'the union' of the Spanish state was holding. The train strike that had just finished was only one other symptom of a wider sickness in the Spanish body politic. This local paper had reported the strike only in the context of how it affected passengers and had given statistics on the percentage of services lost. Apart from mentioning "the failure of the meeting held between workers' representatives and the government minister," it made the unsupported statement that the strike gave a boost to privatisation of the industry.

The newspaper also gave me another unintentional insight into a part of the national psyche (if such a thing can be said to exist.) I detected a distinct, yet soft, tolerance of dictatorship in an editorial about the Moroccan ruler, King Mohammed VI. You can do business with that part of the world, without problems, the editor wrote. The country was "under control" for the last fifteen years. It was "stable and calm," though this column admitted that the Moroccan king had many millions of euros and that national "well-being" only benefited a small minority. In a red brick cafe later in the day the television news told me that Spain was experiencing an increase in domestic violence but a reduction in other crime.

It was not all bad news though. César Bona, a local primary school teacher who teaches in what was termed a "multi-cultural" part of the city, had just been nominated as Spain's entry into this year's million-dollar Global Teacher Prize. In the classroom he was doing many of the kinds of progressive things that are not particularly new in countries with less traditional methods, but compared to those old-fashioned ones that still dominate in almost all Spanish mainstream schools he is a revolutionary. A rare teacher in this country, Mr. Bona has the freedom and courage to barely use text books, give very little homework and run classes that used creativity and respect as the basis of learning, rather than test results and simple memorisation.

Later in the afternoon, while looking for a street in the (now completely gone) old Jewish quarter, I had to take cover in a bar from a second violent storm. A downpour of hailstones a couple of hours earlier had been strong enough to rip posters off walls and make a carpet of nuts, leaves and branches on some stretches of pavement outside my hotel. I could now see why the people from Zaragoza are known as 'maños' (hunchbacks)—the gales can get so strong that you have to walk like Quasimodo, and they can blow in any season, reaching a speed of more than 100 kilometres an hour several times each year. In the second century BC, Cato the Elder had described these as winds "that fill your mouth and tumble wagons and armed men." The soldiers he was referring to were in fact who the town was originally built for. Sometime between 25 BC and 12 BC the emperor Caesar Divi Filius Augustus founded "Caesaraugusta" (from which the modern name "Zaragoza" derives) with a plan to settle Roman legion veterans from the Cantabrian wars.

The winds had now died down and this time when the rain hit again, I sat it out and took shelter from the storm with a *caña* (literally—a cane, such as the sugarcane plant, but also a glass of beer.) My wife called me on my mobile and told me that on the way to England, she had been harassed at Barcelona airport because she didn't have our son's Spanish identity papers in addition to his passport. From an apparently arbitrary decision, this was the first time that either of us had ever been asked for a second form of legal documentation for him to exit or enter the country and she thought she was going to be turned back by the passport control officials. I felt terrible that she had to go through that stressful situation without me, guilty that I was enjoying a stress-free drink while I scribbled in my notebook. Not long after we said goodbye I was cheered up for a few minutes by the comical sight of a tiny Chihuahua outside the bar trying to piss into a pot plant that was too high for it to reach.

When the rain finally passed and evening turned to night I led myself into the narrow-laned *tapas* area called *El Tubo* (literally a tube or pipe, but also translatable as a passageway and even another kind of beer in a glass.) A nurse I knew back home in Vilafranca had told me this was the place to go and I could see the attraction of it immediately. Here was a lack of urban planning that I always enjoyed whenever I encountered it—the same kind of medieval alleys that you find time and time again, albeit in a rougher version, in Morocco's old *souq* markets or *medinas*—human-sized lanes that in some parts would have barely fitted a horse and cart. In today's Zaragoza though—in this dense labyrinth of neon-lit signs and bright shop windows—outside the bars there were crowds of local people chatting next to vintage wine barrels used as tables where smokers could happily drink.

On another night in Zaragoza I ventured into one of those oddities that exist in many medium-sized towns or cities around the world: the English-themed pub. Sitting alone at the bar with her eyes focused on a novel was a young woman. I saw she had light hair and skin and I suspected she might be an Anglo-Brit. After I'd ordered a drink I asked her what she was reading. She told me that the book in her hand was brilliant. It was *Trainspotting* —Irvine Welsh's contemporary stream-of-consciousness tale of Scottish heroin users. I admitted to her that I hadn't read it, but had seen the film version when it had been released in the mid-1990s. From Sheffield in Yorkshire, she was living in the suburbs of the city and working as a nanny/au pair. She told me that her name was Maggie and asked me whether I was also living in Zaragoza. I said I was passing through on my way south, trying to write a travel book. At this, she became animated.

"Wow! I'm thinking about being a writer too," she enthused. "I've already written a novel but I don't want to say nowt (sic) about it now."

I partly understood her reluctance and we talked instead about books and our favourite authors for a while before she stepped outside to have a cigarette. When she came back I bought her a beer and we chatted for a bit more, then Maggie started to talk about her family. She openly told me that her mother was an alcoholic.

"That must have been hard for you at times," I said. "I can empathise with you a bit because my best friend for a long time in

Australia was, and probably still is an alcoholic. He wrote a great book on the ideological battles in philosophy, but in actual fact he was bipolar and was self-medicating with booze and sometimes other drugs. He was never published because the book had been judged to be too dense, according to an editor, and that put him off ever attempting anything again." Maggie looked as if she was thinking about what I'd said for a few seconds and then slipped outside for another cigarette.

"Are you married?" she asked after she had come back to the bar to finish her drink.

"Yes, I am," I replied. "We've been together for a bit over twenty years now. " Before I could say any more she interrupted.

"I'm just amazed how anyone could be in a couple for so long," Maggie gushed. "My parents separated when I was only eight years old and almost all my friends came from one-parent families too. I've only had short relationships with guys. I just don't know how you do it—staying with each other for such a long time. "

When she stepped outside again I struck up a conversation with the barman, a Romanian in his early thirties. He told me he liked Zaragoza very much because he had plenty of friends and that it was a good-sized city—not so big that people didn't know you. "Everyone looks out for each other," he said. This was a pleasant surprise to hear. I knew that some Spaniards lumped in Eastern European migrants with Moroccans ("*Los moros!*") and that they were regularly ill-treated. I asked him if there was ever any trouble in the bar.

"No, not really. We've only needed the police and ambulances a couple of times in the past few years and they get here very quickly. It's almost always tourists who are involved in anything like that," he laughed.

Maggie came back to the bar and finished her drink. Being a modern kind of guy, I proposed that it was now her turn to buy me drink. She claimed to have no money. Maggie had a kind of skitty, feverish intelligence. She had a certain kind of flash in her smile but was somehow delicate like a female subject in a Vermeer painting. I was enjoying talking to her because it was the first conversation I'd had in English for several days so I bought us both another beer. Maggie told me she'd been drinking since the midafternoon. She didn't appear to be inebriated in the slightest.

I have plenty of respect for someone like Maggie. Here she was, doing what many people did not have the guts to do: she was not living in a hermetically-sealed expat community and relying solely on her fellow-Brits for company. Unlike so many of her compatriots, especially those living on the Costa del Sol or the Costa Blanca, Maggie was working, using the language of the land she was a part of. I more or less told her this and left her to chain-smoke through the rest of the night.

In the morning I nosed my way back towards 'The Tube' zone along *El Coso*, a road that follows where a large stretch of the Roman wall once ran, encircling the old town in that typical defensive formation. Against a shopfront was a man squatting. His face was painted with a full clown mask and I took him to be a street performer, like the kind of human statue you often see busking along the Rambla in Barcelona or on Madrid's Gran Via. When I looked a second time I saw him mumbling to himself, hunched over protecting something. It was a Disney Mickey Mouse suitcase.

Around the next corner, in a quiet side street I spotted an old lady sitting with a shopping trolley. Using the wall, she had created a kind of barrier and was setting out her breakfast on the window frame. As I walked by I heard the clinking of a knife and fork and I thought to myself that the day was shaping up somewhat strangely.

A couple of blocks away at the dead end of Calle Veronica, where the day before I had ducked out of the storm, a small street market specialising in local "artisan" producers' wares had sprung up. It was early on a Saturday morning but queues were already forming, despite it being half an hour before the scheduled opening time that was posted on their sign.

Walking on, at the other end of this street were large excavations. An ancient Roman theatre had been unearthed, and just like modern-day Rome itself, it was now home to a colony of cats. It was apparent then that this same area, once also the heart of the Jewish quarter, had been an ancient centre of entertainment. A tomato's throw away is the modern day *Teatro Principal* and only a few minutes' walk up *Plaza Independencia* was yet another theatre displaying posters of international acts who would be performing after the summer. On this street there were also a number of good-looking bookshops—none opening until later in the morning of course—and I took this as another sign of the well-off, middle-class feel to this older part of town. All of this culture pointed to a cultured city.

I was continuing to warm to Zaragoza. The day was warming up too, and in *Plaza Sitio*, a block of land that had formerly been a nuns' convent farm, I came across a relatively rare thing in Spain: a square with plenty of grass in it. The city's main museum, the *Museo del Zaragoza*, was not yet open, so I took my time sitting in the '*parque.*' An oversized column monument stood in its middle. In ultra-dramatic style the sculptor had depicted exhausted, dogged soldiers at its base. Higher up there were screaming women, a General named José Rebolledo de Palafox and figures "representing desperation, pain, hunger and the ruin of war."

At the very top of the statue was the 'heroine' named General Agustina de Aragon. Known as the 'Spanish Joan of Arc,' Agustina was actually born in Reus in Tarragona province. As a lone civilian, she first defended Zaragoza by facing up to the French, firing a cannon into their lines at point blank range in June 1808. Later in her astonishing career, she was to join the allied forces as Wellington's only female officer and ultimately rose to the rank of Captain. Lord Byron was roused. He wrote several highly detailed verses about her in his long narrative poem, *Childe Harold*. I looked at the title of this overbearing work. It was *La Patria* (the homeland) and to me it combined the supposed glory of war with a more truthful study on the agonies of battle.

As if to confirm this impression, behind the monument was a

three-metre-high statue of an exploded grenade—another reminder of Spain's often tragic past. In the square I was also pleased to see something more relevant to my own personal history. A sign next to a small tree proclaimed the World Day of Books and the Rights of the Author. I walked out of the park into a grid of surrounding streets which were straight and wide. Along with the solid stone, formal buildings standing to attention, this sense of composed order gave the area a military feel.

Entry to the grand-looking museum across the street was free. I liked that, and once inside, I roamed through a large, excellent collection of Roman second- and third-century geometric mosaics, the standout being one of a harp player. Apart from Eros and Pan (shown as yet more bloody angels) I was impressed. There was a nicely fleshy marble Venus and a sculpture of a satyr with the head of a Down syndrome child that caught my eye too. The bronze— and Bronze Age—pieces I thought were as good if not better than anything I'd seen in Italy. Quite a few had actually been dug up around Zaragoza itself.

It was now after ten o'clock on this Saturday morning but I was alone here and the rooms were silent. It gave me time and mental space to linger in front of works that interested me. A more contemporary painting titled "Flumen Iberus" stopped me. It showed people swimming in the Ebro River, flush with currents, before the end of the Civil War. The river (just behind the museum) had once been used by locals as an inland beach.

Standing mute, scrutinising this art, I was reminded of one of the main reasons I had first fallen for Europe twenty summers before, when I had made my original three-month visit to this continent. Then, I'd been astounded and inspired by the richness and the variety of the culture that I found in such a relatively small area of the planet. I had studied art history at university the previous year and had backpacked all through Western Europe (but not including Spain) looking to find the originals of many of the creative treasures that I had only seen in books or on slides at lectures. For me, that trip had been the start of my real education

—a sweeping indoctrination into the tangible physical history that, to my mid-twenties psyche, felt more authentic than any Australian expression of consciousness I had come across. It simply said more to me.

This museum, though, was another little gem of a discovery. Here were some superb compositions by local painter Francisco Pradilla Ortiz. Goya too had some nice studies of pale-faced nobles and other folk, including one portrait of a lady in a shawl that looked a lot like my grandmother when she was younger.

In fact, in my daily life I often saw old women in the street who resembled her. Only a few months before a cousin of mine had told me that our grandmother had been led to believe that she was Spanish, on account of her dark, olive skin and unknown father. I had been rocked by this new information, but I also thought that it could possibly explain the long-time infatuation I have had with Iberia as well as a strong attraction that both my twin brother and I have to Morocco, that land of extremes barely a dozen kilometres away across the Gibraltar Strait. Or maybe this was no explanation at all, and I was living here for entirely different reasons. I was being freshly reminded of why Spain means so much to me every hour on the road.

❦ 2 ❦

TO EXTREMADURA

After Zaragoza, I'd thought about going further north up into the province of Burgos to the small mountain town of *Espinosa de los Monteros*. There was a connection here to the great (ex-communicated) Jewish philosopher Baruch Spinoza, whose father was apparently born there. For me, though, the transport connections looked almost as un-promising as they would have been five hundred years ago when Spinoza, one of the forerunners to enlightenment thinking, was just a twinkle in his father's eyes.

Instead, the twinkle of curiosity in my eyes at that moment was when I thought of those long empty plains that lay in wait, stretching 600 kilometres southwest of Zaragoza. From what Catalan people had said to me, Extremadura was a place where few Spaniards bothered to go unless they were driving through it on the way to Portugal. I was just about to learn about how that part of the country was not as empty as I had expected.

At Zaragoza's cavernous, heavily-concreted *Delicias* ("delights") station I hoped to leave and catch a train—any train that would take me close to Extremadura. This was not as simple or as easy as I had expected. It was also more expensive than I had hoped. The only train that went anywhere near where I wanted to go was the high-speed AVE—the *Alta Velocidad Española*. Being summer, the other slower trains which I would have preferred were all booked up and I was peeved to find that I had to be in something called 'tourist plus' class. "Didn't they have a traveller class?" I asked myself in mock indignant silence.

I also needed to wait a few hours. While eating a ham sandwich at one of the station's bars, I saw a young black man reading what I took to be the Koran. He was reciting or memorising lines to himself, mumbling in concentration. I greeted him in Arabic and spoke to him in Castilian Spanish, asking him if what he was doing was difficult. He smiled but did not seem to understand me very well so we then talked in a mixture of French and English. His name was Mohamed Same and he was from Senegal in West Africa.

"I am living in Granada," he said, "and I'm on my way to visit a friend in Seville." He told me he had been studying in Zaragoza and I noticed he only had a small suitcase with him.

"Learning and remembering the entire Koran is a big task, isn't it?" I tried to empathise.

"Oh yes," he agreed and asked me where I was from. When I said Australia he nodded and said "Kangaroos!" which was a common word-association response in Spain.

I shook his hand, touched my heart with my right hand as is the custom, and wished him goodbye with the Arabic words, *ma`a as-salāma*.

I felt a certain degree of kinship with men like these: often solitary and quiet, head in a book or scribbling down thoughts on paper. We are unusual types because Spain is first and foremost a social country where silence among people is much rarer than many other populated places on the planet. Even in an empty cafe or bar there is always, at the least, the TV mounted up on the wall with the volume low. Generally speaking, it is ignored and just goes 'Spanishing on in the background,' as Goytisolo puts it.

In Spain almost never is silence golden. In Seville during my first week visiting the country, while I was sitting at an outdoor cafe in January 1997 a man in his twenties walked up and handed me a printed copy of a poem he had written. It was called "The Silence of the Silence." I have kept it to this day and remember being pleased that he didn't ask any money for it at the time. It reads:

> *El silencio que se toca de sonidos*
> *El sonido que nos habla...*
> *Y en lo lejano, no llega.*
> *El silencio que se alarga de cabida.*
> *El silencio que atrapa el infinito, y la pausa.*
> *El silencio que va hueco con la Nada.*   (*J Esteban y filos. 178*
> *GR/1232/96.)*

In English a translation can be:

The silence that plays off sounds

The sound that speaks to us...

And from so far away, doesn't arrive.

Silence lengthens space.

Silence that traps infinity, and it pauses

The silence that goes hollow with the void.

Spanish people are completely accustomed to continual noise and chatter and often joke about this fact. In truth, many men are openly henpecked by their wives and girlfriends in public. This suggests to me that there must also be a lot of it in private. It's a common enough sight, even in the confines of a train, to witness men being nagged and browbeaten by their partners.

It can start early too. On a train on the way home from Barcelona one night I once watched a couple of no more than fourteen or fifteen years of age. The girl spent a full twenty minutes berating what could only have been her boyfriend. He simply sat with his head down and swallowed his metaphorical medicine. I am sure that this is a pattern of interaction that starts with mother and child and often ends, never deservingly, in explosions of male violence against their female partners.

Before leaving I had a chance to look in Zaragoza's small

station bookshop. There were at least seven titles on the Spanish royal family, in addition to the numerous magazines (such as *Hola*) on which 'the Bourbons'—as they are sometimes called—routinely appear on the cover. I asked the silver-haired man behind the counter for his opinion about why they were so popular, but he hadn't listened to me, instead saying in an angry tone the equivalent of "What a pain in the neck!" He then charged out to the shelves to show me the very same books I had just asked him about.

Now, away from aggression, and apparently much safer in a train that was set to exceed 300 kilometres an hour, I took my reserved seat. I was reluctantly riding on the Spanish version of Japan's '*shinkansen*,' known as the 'bullet trains.' (Near where I lived I regularly saw the special blue fence rails that run marking the various AVE paths and had thought that I would never be on one.) To my surprise, there was security screening before the platform, including uniformed hostess-style staff X-raying all passenger baggage. Similarities with airline travel did not end there. The train ticket itself looked more like a boarding pass for an Iberia Airways flight. And I quickly found that writing in my notebook made me queasy from the speed of the train with its constantly rattling carriages—these felt like being in synthetic dozing chambers when compared to the experience of most other Spanish railways I'd spent time on, where there is often a more social atmosphere.

The AVE's continued existence was itself very controversial. As my friend, long-time Catalan resident Matthew Tree had written in one of his articles:

"Since 1992, governments of both the right and left have spent €50,000 million of public money on line after line, each radiating out of the Spanish capital, so that now Spain... has more kilometres of high-speed rail than any other country except China."

At least the expense of this seat made it a comfortable one and there was much more legroom than on an airplane. Looking at the view from the window at first was uninspiring. One after another:

chain burger outlets, chain supermarkets, a chain cinema; more chains than watching *Twelve Years a Slave*. Up close, the landscape was a '*flashby quick*,' parched blur. We were racing through flat, squat towns—all too fast to get a sense of what they actually looked like. The changing speed of the train was shown on a digital chronometer: 247 km/hour, then 299 km/hour, and the sheer rapidity of movement created an irritating expectation in me that I would be in Madrid very soon, even though I knew that I was hours away.

Next to me a man was filming his sleeping wife. Near them a little white Maltese dog in a cage yapped and yapped. Directly in front of me, a young woman in very short cutoff jeans began to fuss over the pet. I noticed that the backs of her upper thighs showed tattoos with Native American dream weaver patterns and on her arms were tiger paw prints and birds that looked like swallows. She was travelling with other, older females who had the family resemblance of relatives. For something to do—I couldn't read—I counted how many times the dog was (unsuccessfully) told to sit, now that it was out of its tiny little metal cage, but I stopped bothering to add up when I got to ten after a few minutes.

Outside in the far distance, despite the high speed, on this clear day it was easy to make out fast-rising ranges of peaks. It's never long at all before you see mountains in Spain, probably because it is the most mountainous country in Europe. To the left of the train across the province of Castile-La Mancha I had a view of the Caldereros range. At the far end of it is the Castillo de Zafra, a startling and angular thirteenth-century castle built on a wide monolith of natural stone. Recently called "something out of a JRR Tolkien fever dream" as an attraction, it was soon destined to be become more popular. The producers of the hit TV show *Game of Thrones* were planning to use it for their "Tower of Joy" in an upcoming season.

This speeding train was now raised on its line, moving at the top of low hills and then boring its way through them. Regardless of the twists and turns and curves of the earth, it seemed as if we were heading in a straight line that was opening up these reddish purple patches of lavender fields, occasional yellow sunflowers and wheat-coloured plains. Just before getting into the first and penultimate stop at Guadalajara I could see a large range of mountains that included the *Sierra de Guadarrama*. It was across some of these that Catholic groups were planning to put thirteen hundred crosses, each one standing four metres tall.

At the next stop I was to change trains. Somewhat fittingly, being the main station in the main city, Madrid's *Atocha* station is an embodiment of the best and worst of Spain. Four months earlier had marked the tenth anniversary of a rapid series of commuter train bombings in and near the station. These explosions had killed almost 200 people and injured one thousand eight hundred. Then, four days away from an election, conservative Prime Minister José Maria Aznar had ignored clear evidence of Al Qaeda involvement and immediately tried to blame the Basque separatist terrorist group named ETA.

To this day, many Spaniards—including some of the survivors—are certain that Aznar lied to them, and in a huge upset his party was immediately voted out of office. Amongst a mix of tragedy and great courage, the nation's leaders had once again let the people down.

Attempting to find my connecting express service to my destination of Mérida was also a kind of microcosm of living in this country. I searched the massive station for quarter of an hour, growing more exasperated by the minute that I couldn't find the correct area. I saw that the building was in fact a number of buildings cobbled together and, just like Madrid itself (and most other Spanish towns and cities), there had been precious little forward planning. New wings had just been added on when required. This lack of organised forethought had created what I discerned as at least four distinct parts to the station: a raised area for the AVE, a tunnel off to the city's extensive underground *metro* system, the local train *(cercanias)* platforms and the "medium distance" lines which I now needed to get to in a hurry.

Despite a complete absence of helpful signs, I somehow came across an information desk. Naturally, there was a long line of people waiting. When my turn eventually came to ask where I could find my train, two young South American women stepped in front of me and started talking to the young guy at the desk. I objected to him, but was dismissed with a casual wave of the hand. Ignoring a queue is a common enough practice in Spain, but it is usually done by old ladies who say something like *"Una preguntita:"* ("I just have a little question.") I had been well and truly *preguntita-ed* and was in danger of missing the last train to Mérida for the day.

Just as with Spain's history, *Atocha* station also had some dark corners and temporary corridors. With its low ceilings too it reminded me of the old Heathrow airport, but without as much palpable tension. The place where I and the other passengers sat waiting for trains appeared to be untouched since the 1970s: geometric panels of garish red, pink and purple covered one wall and on another there were multiple layers of grey-brown slate tiles. Just being there made me feel odd, as if I was eight years old again and expecting my mother to come out of the deli with slices of silverside for my twin brother and me to eat.

It occurred to me as I sat there making my notes that writing can be a way to dull the ache of waiting and at times to even make sense of our surroundings, especially when they are new. When we observe, not merely look, we defeat that state of listlessness that is so often (wrongly) called boredom. Our species arguably has only two states of being: occupied or unoccupied. It is the unoccupied individual who can succumb to tedium, but here it was more than just that keeping people restless and shuffling in their seats. The cramped space severely lacked air. Several older women fanned themselves, cooling down and re-directing unused energy. To distract myself, I thought of Spain's complex language of *abanico* fan hand signals that is still understood by a number of today's Andalusian women—a poetic, romantic form of communication where subtly moving an open or closed fan can mean anything from "I want to see you," to "I'm thinking about it" or even an emotional "Leave me alone, I am upset."

Personally, I was a long way from upset when the train finally pulled in, then readied to pull out. It had been a trial in this disorientating station; the kind of scene that visits you again in sweaty nightmares: you're running late and the roof is pressing down on your head. You weave through the jostling hordes trying without success to avoid catching sight of their tense, hungering faces; all the while, the sensation of wandering lost in a strange place, then bracing yourself against the cold, arbitrary treatment by uniformed officials, and spitting out a bitter phlegm at being cheated.

Leaving *Atocha* as a pardoned man, I started again on Goytisolo's autobiography. He was comparing a few of his older relatives' fixed beliefs in an afterlife with that of the Egyptian nobles, as well as their simplistic division of a world of religious good and evil. Outside, it was not quite as dry as the Pharaoh's Valley of the Dead, but signs of life were almost as few.

At a consistent speed of 152 km/hour—half the speed of the AVE fast train I'd been on a few hours earlier—I could see details clearly as we rolled across the flatlands of Castile-La Mancha. One of the first ever Spanish novels, *The Life of Lazarillo de Tormes*, was set in this region (often called "the bread basket of Spain") and the small medieval city of Toledo just to the east of the train line. The author of this once royally-banned but still popular picaresque tale is unknown, but Juan Goytisolo supports the claim that it was penned by Alfonso de Valdes, who came from a converted Jewish background and took on the post of Latin secretary to the then emperor.

The book (which is prescribed reading for my son and other secondary school students across the country) has a strong feel of Dickens about. A young itinerant Lazaro moves from master to master and town to town "as chance dictates," mainly attempting to put an end to his constant hunger. Reading his exploits, we witness a Spain where priests beat their child slaves and keep the bread locked away from them. As well, it is the Spain of blind beggars being paid by the rich to say their prayers for them while those same 'nobles' buy papal indulgences.

It is these same 'barren high plains of Castile' and their 'heroic light' that opens the first pages of Barcelona author Eduardo Mendoza's jaunty, airy novel, *An Englishman in Madrid*. His main character is escaping by train from a love affair and stumbles into a conglomeration of intricacies in the build-up to the Spanish Civil War. At least I was doing neither of these two things and was instead getting away from Madrid.

The first time I'd visited the city was in the winter of 1997 and it had frozen me to the bone. In the hotel I'd been forced to learn the Spanish words for lukewarm (*calido*) and hot (*caliente*) after the shower only produced water that barely resembled anything a shower should. There too, I learnt the word for early (*temprano*) owing to someone vacuuming outside the room at six in the morning. My partner Paula and I had also finally run out of money in Madrid (after our bank card had been swallowed by a cash machine in Morocco a few weeks earlier) and we had spent a full day in the bitter cold without eating. The previous day had been Seinfeldian. Without success, we had searched the whole damned city for hours, desperately hunting for a large airline regulation cardboard box for our heavy North African *tagine* pot.

Despite all that personal history of drudgery, I had kept a good impression of Madrid. That is until I revisited it during Spain's successful football World Cup win in 2010. To my surprise, I found that streets and squares I had remembered favourably were now ugly, dirty and unappealing—only partly because of the badly polluted air. City council cuts to street cleaning and other essential services had become severe and the following year one organisation found that Madrid was in fact one of the nation's three dirtiest major towns.

Many *Madrileños* also soon became appalled and embarrassed by their (appointed/unelected) mayoress Ana Botella, wife of the former conservative Prime Minister, José María Aznar. Famously, she gave a speech in English to international Olympic committee delegates in support of Madrid's bid for the games in 2020, but had instead caused a huge public backlash. Having lost in its fourth successive attempt to capture the right to hold the Olympics, Botella—and Botella only—copped the blame.

As part of her speech the mayoress had said, in an intentional mix of English and Castilian Spanish, that "there's nothing quite like (having) a relaxing cup of cafe con leche" in the capital's main square, the Plaza Mayor. It was this short phrase that caught on in the public mind, being brief enough to spread widely and wildly through social media. Within a couple of days, a satirical YouTube video had gone viral and T-shirts with a parody of the Starbucks logo along with a profile of Botella and her new catchphrase were selling at eighteen euros each.

At the time I publicly wrote that her political views and plenty of public statements—especially her anti-gay rhetoric—were objectionable but, after actually watching the speech, I thought it was no major disaster. It could have been quite a bit better, of course, given the audience. As if she had been one of my struggling adult students, I simply tried to take a fair attitude towards her (though Botella herself was well-known for her unfairness), and I did this because she was speaking a second language in a public forum. Yes, she spoke with an accent (as, in truth, we all do) but I understood every word and she seemed to me to be sincere in her enthusiasm about the city. She had to simplify things—which her conservative party is particularly good at doing—and her statement that Madrid is "full of welcoming people" was somewhat debatable, but she had a good point about the rich culture of the city. I'm sure Botella still lives her life with a disgusting amount of privileges thrown her way, but getting plenty of good English learning was obviously not one of them.

I am always in favour of holding individuals in power to account over their words and actions, but I would think that her record as Mayor has a lot more in it to criticise than one border-line average speech. Many of the Catalans I know were especially mocking of Botella. In that deep historical Madrid/Barcelona rivalry she was the butt of jokes, but even the people of her city stopped supporting her in the opinion polls. Despite a pledge to run for re-election in 2015, she was forced out of the candidacy by her *Partido Popular* colleagues. Perhaps unsurprisingly, the candidate they chose to replace her, a woman named Esperanza Aguirre, who had previously been mayoress for a nine-year period, also found herself the centre of controversy. In a move that would be illegal in Spain, she said she wanted to sweep the homeless off the streets to help tourism.

In truth, I was not the only visitor to Madrid to be underwhelmed. In the late 1800s, Frenchman Eugène Poitou (like me) had travelled there from Zaragoza, which he thought to be the most interesting city of Spain, but found the capital to be "deficient in charm and grandeur." He saw it in the same way as many people have told me they see Canberra—my city of birth—as "an artificial creation living with a facetious life." Poitou put this down to Madrid being the royal court, so therefore neither the real "head nor the heart of the country." Others have mocked its Manzanares River for being an "apprentice stream," but my complaints are less poetic and more prosaic.

I later read about a man named Edu who had started off to do the trip I was about to do, but in reverse, and on foot. Fresh out of prison, he had left Madrid the previous spring thinking he would need about three weeks to reach his destination. On the first night, though, he had escaped the cold by wandering into terminal four of the capital's Barajas Airport and has in fact stayed there ever since then. Along with at least thirty other homeless people, they are all reportedly tolerated by the authorities provided that they don't cause trouble inside the building.

But here now, more than 100 kilometres away from 'The Royal City,' the train passed seemingly unnoticed and without stopping through a small village named *Alberche del Caudillo*. It had been inaugurated as a new town in the mid-1950s as one of eight towns that have still kept in their name the word Caudillo (meaning *The Leader*, i.e., Francisco Franco, Spain's military dictator from 1939-

1975). This drowsy little place is continuing to defy a post-Franco law that "is unequivocal about the obligation to remove references to (him) from street names and plaques, while place names remain ambiguous."

Today, chance dictated that for my amusement on the train, half a dozen rows in front of me, a young, fair-skinned girl with sandy hair was having fun popping her head up and down above the seats. She was a Down syndrome child and had an infectious 'hee hee' laugh which showed that her top front teeth were missing, and this added to her cuteness. She moved confidently around the carriage chatting to anyone she felt like and ended up finding a young woman working on a laptop computer opposite me. There was an empty seat next to her, and both of them hit it off immediately, talking and joking as if they were old friends. The little girl said her name was Marta and quickly took a liking to pounding on the buttons of her new playmate's laptop keyboard. The woman repeatedly tried to show her how to type her own name but Marta had no interest in that. She apparently already knew that a computer was an important object, but used it as a source of conversation rather than anything else. Then, Marta's mother called her away back to her seat. Marta pointedly ignored this request. From the other end of the carriage her father had been constantly watching and he came to get her, calmly telling her to stop bashing her hands on the computer.

"YOU stop!" Marta blurted, defiantly.

Quietly and patiently her father spoke to her, in a voice that I couldn't hear well enough to understand. He distracted his daughter and took her back to her mother. Soon, with a hairbrush, Marta started to tend to her father's hair, roughly dragging the bristles up and down his scalp in a preening gesture, as if he was one of her unfeeling dolls. This activity calmed her down and before long she was asleep on her mother's lap.

In enjoying Marta's adorable antics I had done what many Spanish people habitually do. I used my surroundings to pass the time, and if it was a social interaction, all the better. Many people in Spain will openly stare at others and not see it as at all rude. (And was this also a European-wide custom?)

Now though, the light had changed. Disappearing behind the tail of the train lay the wind-blown town of *Oropesa* (loosely translatable as *gold weight*). One of the fields did in fact take on an almost luminous, golden yellow, and I thought of Jack Kerouac's *"rolls and gold folds"* and his maker saying *unto him:*

"Go thou across the ground; go moan for man; go moan, go groan, go groan alone, go roll your bones, alone; go thou and be little beneath my sight; go thou, and be minute and as a seed in the pod,... go thou... and of this world report you well and truly."

I liked Kerouac's god ordering him to report the world both well and truly. This could easily have been my sole commandment. In my earthly world it was summer. But if I'd been travelling through this area in spring I would have made a small detour to the Jerte Valley near *Cáceres* (winner of the 2015 Culinary City of Spain competition, incidentally). It would be quite something to see more than two million soft pink-white cherry trees blossoming. If the Japanese learnt of this they would surely go there in droves to make comparisons with their own *sakura* season.

But that all-too-short ten-day period in March was long gone and, swerving around a hill, a vast body of water suddenly appeared —a statement of abundance and life in this hard land, like something biblical from a Leonard Cohen song. This was the *Embalse de Valdecañas* that marks the start of Extremadura province, being connected to the more than 1,000-kilometre-long Tajo (or Tagus) river that sweeps into Portugal: a river that two millennia ago the Roman poet Ovid sang the praises of for its gold-bearing sands.

Time passed slowly. From the train window I saw an apartment block sitting incongruously in the middle of one of the fields. It made me remember a newly non-Communist rural Czech Republic, where I'd been twenty summers earlier. Next was another broad field, this one stretched with neat rows of silver solar panels.

Apart from this, the landscape might be unfairly described as featureless. But it was not as monotonous as a great deal of southern Australia, for example. Here today were drooping sunflowers, shaped like an army of question marks, leaning and facing up to their source of sustenance. Over there: part trees, part bushes pimpling the almost imperceptible undulation, a dark bank of mountains off behind. I could see why men had once hidden in those *sierra*. There was nowhere else for cover on this vast table-top. My mind pictured rabbits zig-zagging again and memory insisted that this place resembled the parched landscape around *Alberobello* in Italy's deprived Puglia region.

After a while a herd of sturdy black bulls came into sight—that muscular symbol of the nation—right beside the train, all of them just like the sunflowers, looking in the same direction as if facing their own collective bovine Mecca. What soon followed was kilo-metre after kilometre of gnarly trees that I thought must be cork or oak. When I spotted piles of dry shavings next to them I realised that most of those were in fact cork—some being hundreds of years old—with their red-brown lower regions bare of bark. The grass around looked exactly like the kind that wildfire could race through in a high wind. In fact, a decade earlier the European Union—not any Spanish government—had given 1.3 million euros from a "Solidarity Fund" to pay for extreme forest fire damage in the *San Vicente de Alcántara* region just south of here.

At *Cañaveral*, the train skirted the little town, opening up to abandoned buildings in the empty twilight of an expanse of hori-zon. We twisted through low hills with mossy rock outcrops behind eucalyptus-like trees, then surprisingly, in the uncluttered moment, I am aware that I'm going somewhere with almost no expectations. I have no map, no schedule and am letting only my eyes tell me where I am. This land is far from the vacant nonentity that people had suggested would be here. It feels open and spacious, certainly, but not a geographical vacuum.

The word empty had often been ascribed to Extremadura, but I originally come from Australia, a so-called "Empty Continent" of *terra nullius*: a Roman term used by the British to conveniently ignore the indigenous inhabitants and declare the entire continent as "nobody's land." I had been to the outback desert of Australia, where you can drive for hours without seeing a living soul. That to me was genuine emptiness. And genuine happiness.

I love wide stretches of free land, but to the average Spaniard, who typically thrives in company and is most at home in a crowd, these fields of Extremadura (which literally means "extremely tough") could even be intimidating, only partly because not far back in time there were bandits in the region. They were named as the 'extreme' end of the country. If it is at least not totally empty, there is certainly a sense of that great lonesome feeling created by the far-off, long, long line at which the earth's surface and the sky meet: a pleasant melancholy of an imagined solitary truck crawling across a plain, the ancestral memory of a caravan trail or a child's drawing of a single emblematic tree on a small hill.

This was my testimony of one human sitting still on a train: all this against a surprise grey sky, and I thought, 'I am where a very long time ago the Spanish mainland had been connected with Africa. Here, the tectonic plates had, inch by creaking inch, separated two continents by a sea.'

৯৫৯

PURELY BY COINCIDENCE, ON THIS NIGHT I HAPPENED TO ARRIVE in Mérida while a festival was on. The town was buzzing with people, many having come to see performances at the town's UNESCO listed Roman Theatre, as part of the 60th Mérida International Classical Theatre Festival.

The crowds, some even dressed in togas and others in formal wear, were almost entirely heading in one direction: up the hill to what was claimed to be "the oldest theatre in the world to host performances of classical texts." In the throng I twice heard the word 'patrimonio' (meaning heritage or legacy) being spoken, but I wasn't there to pay to watch Shakespeare done in Castilian Spanish, and I had hunger prevailing through my innards, anyway. I prowled up and down the strip trying to use my instincts for a good restaurant, bypassing the outdoor tables and their pockets of cigarette smoke.

Finally choosing a noisy, crowded tapas bar I was given the only vacant table for one, right next to the toilet. I ordered the cheapest dish that had the simple name of '*carne y tomate*' and as soon as I tried it, found it to be one of the most tender meat stews I'd ever eaten, thick and rich with the flavour of tomato and sweet smoked paprika. It was served alongside superb hand-cut chips, and the size of it all was more than plentiful. I drank a glass of dry house white wine; a tired traveller, savouring the atmosphere where people of all ages were meeting, chatting, drinking and eating together - exemplifying that Spanish brand of conviviality in public places that they do so extraordinarily well.

After deciding that my introduction to the food of Extremadura could not have been better, I turned off the main drag, and it was quickly apparent that I was leaving all the life behind. With no map, I picked my way through the quiet back streets of the town and ended up where I started, having seen barely a soul. Back at my stuffy, windowless hotel room I tried the TV, but it refused to work. I was reminded that travel, or at least the improvised way I do it, can be a rollercoaster ride.

At breakfast in a bar the next morning I had natural orange juice that was naturally sweet, though still served with a little sachet of sugar, as was the national custom. There was flamenco music on the TV and already in the streets outside there was the uplifting sight of girls singing together while they walked along. Catalans had warned me again and again about the heat in this region, but until about midday it felt cool at twenty-three degrees. Outside, when I asked, a local woman told me that at this time of year it's usual for the weather to have a pleasant spring feeling in the morning.

Freshly energised, I ambled, now with a map, across town to the *Circo Romano*, one of the biggest "race tracks" (as they translated it) in the Roman world, able to hold thirty thousand citizens. Oddly, it was not possible to buy a single entrance ticket. Visitors are obliged to pay twelve euros for a combined pass to four of Mérida's different '*monumentos*.' Sensing a rip off, I walked out of the entrance and instead looked through a hole in the fence at the old running track—a brown, open patch of dirt with a few remaining stone walls.

Across a busy road I took a longer gaze (also for free) at the *Milagros* aqueduct, its mighty spanning double arches mostly still well-preserved. At 830 metres in length and 25 metres high, it is a particularly impressive feat of engineering and a more than practical way to have brought water coursing into the old city from the Proserpine Lake over seven hundred years ago.

Through a section of its curves passes the *Albarregas* River (or *Barraeca,* as it was called in Roman times, when it was used as a sewer). Today, it had the green slime of something like a modern outdoor sewer drain and trickled calmly, rather than ran. When I looked closer I could see small holes that had been made all along the base of the aqueduct wall.

This was a clever way of relieving any buildup of water pressure, ensuring that the great big thing would not collapse. In front were low remains of some Roman baths. A sign said that these were completely abandoned after four hundred years of use. Behind this I could see three ancient pillars with stork nests on top. On the way into town from the train the other day I had seen a couple of them there too, '*in full proprietorial dignity, each perched on one leg like a fakir.*'

As a child, the great American author John Steinbeck had been inspired by a scene with a stork. He cherished a toy 'Easter looking-egg' which he loved to peer into through a tiny hole, seeing "a lovely little farm, a kind of dream farm, and on the farmhouse chimney a stork sitting on a nest." Steinbeck had taken this setting to be pure fantasy, but to his surprise saw the same thing in real life one day in Denmark.

My own young imagination, before I could even read, had been fired by books like Margaret Wise Brown's *Scuppers The Sailor Dog*, with its superbly memorable illustrations by Garth Williams. I'd always ask my mother to read me this story and one scene in particular is imprinted on my memory even still. Like Steinbeck, I'm sure that it fed my unconscious with a deep desire to travel.

Brave Scuppers is asleep in a warm bunk bed in his cosy, wood-paneled ship's cabin. The ship is tossing because I can see that the light is swinging from the roof, and outside through the round porthole window, the sea is choppy. Under his bed are his new shoes that he picked out from a shop on the previous page. Scuppers rejected a pair as being 'too fancy' because they were curly at the toe ends.

This shop (where he also bought a 'bushel' of oranges) had palm trees outside and a woman in a veil walking by, seemingly in a hurry. I'd never seen either of those things before and didn't know the word 'exotic' then, but that's what I was thinking in my forming child's outlook. When I got to Morocco twenty-five years later and saw the same curly shoes that Scuppers had passed over, I felt what must have been a similar, satisfying surprise as John Steinbeck had once enjoyed.

Consciously, my love affair with travelling on trains began exactly two decades earlier when my partner Paula and I spent over three months on different forms of them getting across Europe. As a child and young adult I'd barely been on a train before, but there was something either in my ancestral memory or a different kind of spark that kindled a vague interest in a different sort of transport aside from buses or planes. Maybe it was hearing Neil Diamond on TV when I was eight years old. I still recall him singing:

It's a beautiful noise
Goin' on ev'rywhere
Like the clickety-clack
Of a train on a track
It's got rhythm to spare

In this song too, he poeticised the sounds of the big city street as music to the ear, and my budding brain was intrigued by this idea. Living in quiet suburbia where the high-pitched *ninga-ninga* of summer lawn mowers was the most common weekend noise, I'd never heard anything like the kind of thing in Diamond's lyrics and was touched by his clear affection for the pulse and grind of the metropolis. It has stayed with me in the same way that thoughts on a train trip from over twenty years ago will now and then float back into memory.

Travel has a way of also emboldening us because we are out of the realm of home's familiar touches. Under the stork nest near Mérida's ancient aqueduct, I started talking to a middle-aged man who was walking two schnauzer dogs. He told me there were big problems with his job at the local university (using the word *problemon*) and that times were also hard for others in his family, including his brother, who was twenty-three and still lived at home with their parents. "He can't become independent," he said solemnly, looking at the ground.

I stopped and asked another man about some flowers that were growing down from a wall over the footpath along a nearby main road. '*Jazmín*,' he called them, but I recognised them as honeysuckle vines—those fragrant beauties that you can pull the stamen from and suck sweet nectar off. When I told the old man about how, as kids in Australia, my brothers and I used to do that, he nodded, "Ah yes, we did that too."

Further on beside the ruins of the former '*termas*' or hot springs, was a massive, fenced-off archaeological dig in progress. It was as large as two football fields, surrounded by modern-day houses. Right here, in the very middle of the town, something was being newly discovered, albeit slowly. I was starting to get the impression (just as Richard Ford—the son of a London police chief —did back in 1832) that Mérida was a mini-Rome in the making. Just as with parts of Italy, you keep stumbling across bits of the long-distant past.

It was hotter now. I'd drunk all my water and stopped for a beer at a little kiosk on an open square where children were playing. I asked the owner how business was. "The crisis is still here," he stated matter-of-factly, and refilled my water bottle from a tap behind the bar, refusing any money for doing so. Further on, I loitered outside the beautiful old white painted courthouse, noticing that it still had bars on its ground floor windows. Heading downhill, I passed a butchery given the name of a man that translates as John Vinegar. Then I saw another stork—I'd been told they'd probably be gone by this time of year—this one with a long supervisor's neck, aptly perched on the top of the observatory building. Here, down a side street, some graffiti told me in Castilian Spanish that "if we don't have a future, we don't have fear."

Now the town was quiet and few people were getting about. I wandered along an old street with the charming name of *Almendralejo* (a nearby 'almond' town). Coming to the bottom of a hill, I reached a powerful and wide river, the *Rio Guadiana*. I could see two bridges—an old one off a few hundred metres to my left, and closer, this modern one with a long arch spanning it, as if the trajectory of an arrow fired from one river bank had been traced to the other. This is the Lusitania Bridge, its name having been taken from the conquered and then partly enslaved (Indo-European) Lusitanian people. Lusitania was the title given to the Iberian Roman province that once included roughly all of modern Portugal south of the Douro River and modern day Extremadura. Mérida had been its capital city, and like Zaragoza, it had been set up as a place specifically for veteran soldiers, though it had been given two public forums, not just one as was customary. At that time the town was known as *Augusta Emerita*, where we get today's term 'Emeritus scholar' from.

I walked on and crossed the pedestrian path of this half-kilometre construction. It was like walking under a canopy of oversized vertical knitting needles. Valencian neo-futuristic architect and structural engineer Santiago Calatrava designed the bridge in the early 1990s. Internationally known, especially for the spectacular designs of his sensuously curved steel and glass buildings at the *Ciudad de las Artes y las Ciencias* in the capital of his region, Calatrava has also shaped a number of railway stations, including the

World Trade Center Transportation Hub at the rebuilt World Trade Center in New York City. As is almost customary for a wealthy and well-known Spaniard, he has been the centre of controversy, in his case for overcharging the Valencian government. Along with three other engineers he is currently facing court proceedings for the same offence relating to a bridge he worked on in Venice.

Noting the hideous, grey, lego block, square box of the *Palacio de Congresos*—clearly not one of Calatrava's works—I walked in the opposite direction through dry-grass parks along the west bank of the river, eventually coming to where the old Roman bridge began. Sitting next to an old white-painted well was a middle-aged man with long, dark hair. He was singing loud enough to be heard from the other side of the road: a lovely, strong but sweet flamenco trill. I walked over to him.

"I couldn't help hearing you from over there," I said, pointing off to the old town. "You have a beautiful voice. Very authentic."

"That's kind of you," he said, and looking directly into my eyes he gave me another short burst of song.

"What is that song about?" I asked.

"Oh, we sing about a lot of different themes. I am a Gypsy. All our songs explore universal things: happiness, jealousy, death, grief."

I asked him about '*duende*,' the spirit of flamenco, and what it means to him personally. "It's the motivation, a feeling that's essential to the music." I told him I'd recently been listening to a flamenco singer from Barcelona named Mayte Martin and that I thought she also had a wonderful voice.

"Ah yes," he said, "I have sung on the same stage as her." He listed a number of other names that I hadn't heard of and stated that he had toured France a number of times. As with many other flamenco singers, his biggest influence and hero was the Gypsy '*El Camarón*' (nicknamed The Shrimp.) Did he agree, I wondered, with the theory that his people had originally come India?

"Yes, that is documented. The Punjab, the military campaign, then one group went off to Eastern Europe and another here." It's generally accepted that Gypsy migration from India to Europe was still continuing as recently as the 11th century. He also agreed with me that the oral tradition and very little written history is a feature of their culture. "That is why we sing. To explain. My family originated in Extremadura. I have four children and my father at home here but I have a brother living in Barcelona."

"I live in Barcelona too, but I'm from Australia," I said. "I'm travelling through the region and further on."

"I've been to Australia once. I liked it. I lived in a 'chalet' there and sang in Sydney and Melbourne, but I don't speak much English and only a little French."

"Did you have any problems with racism there or here in Spain?"

"Well, people can be afraid if they don't know you. We face the stereotype of being thought of as thieves, but the bigger difficulty from day to day is unemployment."

I told this friendly, talkative man that I was going to the Andalusian town of Jaen in a few days. "Oh, watch out for the sun on your head there. It gets very hot." This, to me, was a Spanish, even Mediterranean statement. The heat is always worse somewhere else, just as for an Italian no town is ever as lovely as their hometown.

Now that he had to go to meet his wife, he told me his name was Juan de Pura. I asked him if he had a website and he referred me to YouTube, where he has several videos. Juan would be singing at the *Peña Flamenca* in Córdoba the following month, he said. We shook hands and wished each other good luck and Juan sauntered off home through the park singing, this time almost only to himself. I recalled how I'd first heard the strong tones of his voice from across the street and couldn't help thinking of a Bob Dylan line: "Bird on the horizon sitting on a fence. He's singing a song for me at his own expense."

I liked Juan and his openness, but the truth is that he and his fellow Gypsies are still widely misunderstood. Also known in

English as Roma, Romani, Sinti and Askali, across the entire continent their history has often been a blighted one. A recent report by George Soros' Open Society Institute acknowledged that their 600-year existence in Spain has shown only small signs of being slightly more tolerated over the last couple of decades, compared with other EU nations. It is undeniably the case, though, that Gypsies still "face disadvantages and...significant barriers" in schooling, (literacy), employment, housing, general health and life expectancy." It was also found that the country's estimated 800,000 gypsies—40 per cent live in Andalucía—make up to 90 per cent of the shanty-town dwellers.

In popular literature Gypsies have largely been caricatured in a simplistic way. Writing a short story in 1613, Cervantes, the author of *Don Quixote* and Spain's most famous writer, fictionalised Gypsies into figures such as a "cunning grandmother" with a beautiful dancer daughter and poets who "condescend to deal with (them.)" A century ago, the missionary George Barrow encountered a Roma baby with his mother in Seville. He recorded the baby as looking "sly and wicked."

In the wider consciousness the Roma are usually linked with thievery and crime, as Juan pointed out to me, and like many stereotypes there is a degree of truth to that. Gypsy families dominate the cocaine trade in Barcelona as well as other parts of the continent, and their children across Europe have long been used by their parents to pickpocket the gullible. Roma women are particularly overrepresented in Spanish prison populations, leading Gypsy spokesmen to acknowledge that there is a culture of "dependency" in their communities. This, despite a Gypsy belief that they "are considered neither a Spanish nor an immigrant community but something entirely different, and that is the way (we) are treated."

The idea that the fundamental difference between Gypsies and non-Gypsies is an ethnic one was shockingly illustrated by a reactionary Catalan industrialist in Emilio Calderon's novel of 2006, *The Creator's Map*. This character always carried an article in his pocket from the Catalan Nationalist newspaper *La Nació* from 1934, in which he had underlined the following sentence: "We have never wanted to belong to the Spanish state because the smell of gypsies disgusts us."

In a much more even-handed way, Isabel Fonseca's penetrating non-fiction work, *Bury Me Standing*, brought into sharp view the ultra-close-knit lives of the Roma in modern Eastern and Central Europe. At times living with them, Fonseca showed that, whether settled or on the move, there is a strict (originally Hindu-based) moral code where men and women are clearly separated. In Mikey Walsh's autobiography *Gypsy Boy*, he illustrates how fierce interclan violence is routinely used in Britain. Contrary to common belief, many Roma tend to be entrepreneurial by nature, though not always within the strict bounds of the law. Car dealing is a common male occupation and Gypsy women in Albania have also been known to dabble in currency speculation.

The Gypsies, of course, are inseparable with music, and especially flamenco music. According to James Woodall, who wrote *Firedance*, the first detailed English language book on the subject, the word *flamenco* "might be of Arab derivation—*felamengu* means fugitive peasant, (and) *fela men eikum* (was a word for) an Andalusian worker of the Muslim occupation." In addition to that, *Fellahin* is a type of Egyptian folkloric belly-dancing which flamenco dance can be reasonably compared with, in my view. The mistaken assumption that Gypsies were in fact Egyptians comes directly from *gitano*—the Spanish word given to them.

For anyone who has experienced authentic flamenco with an open mind, it can be something genuinely phenomenal.

Not being at all a fan of dance, I was captivated and emotionally moved the first time I saw a performance of it live on stage in Australia, many years before I felt compelled to come and live here. The musicians and dancers were a small group that travelled the world, and what astonished me as much as anything else were the dancers. I'd never seen such ultra-confidence and casual arrogance so clearly expressed through the body, and this from women to the same high degree as the men. It impressed me too that some of the curvaceous female dancers were over forty-five years of age—a time of life when so much of the western world's media has seemed to decide that women's bodies should be ignored or airbrushed into near-pubescent perfection.

Having said goodbye to the singer Juan, and feeling thrilled at having met him completely from blind luck, I started out across the eighty-one arches of the old Roman bridge. In the late 1930s Gertrude Bone wrote that halfway across this '"relentless" bridge she had felt as if she'd been in "an ordeal by sunlight, unable to turn back, caught in a 'forced march (with) horses, oxen, carts, donkeys (and) men." But today, in the mid-afternoon summer it was almost deserted, save for a couple of joggers with earphones on, crossing its rough time-worn cobblestones. Over on the far bank I could see the town again but under me, what seemed at first like two separate rivers I realised was actually a long man-made mini island used to divert currents.

Being a cheapskate, I chose to head uphill for a bit more culture that cost no money, merely time. I passed the only remaining Moorish wall—there was an absurd cover charge to get into a display on the other side of it—and further on found myself inside Mérida's Roman Art Museum. It was cool, spacious and had several levels to it given over to piece after piece that, with their detail, testified to the respect and fascination for living creatures that existed in their former empire. In one exquisite fourth century mosaic (measuring a huge 10.8 metres high by 8.5 metres wide), a wild boar with its back arched and front legs splayed in the air is powerfully resisting a hunter who has just jammed a spear into the animal's bleeding neck. Nearby, in two bronzes (the kind apparently found all throughout many Roman houses) movement is also given voice in the straining muscles of a galloping horse: a static form full of life.

Reaching out from the centuries there was gentle humour too: I was tickled by a depiction of some dogs climbing on each other while biting the leg of the dog above. Even a single little bronze shin guard from a soldier statute was on display in an understated way, but the skill of the workmanship staggered me, considering that it was crafted before machine tools were barely even dreamt of. This was part of a collection of over a dozen bronzes. I'd never seen such quality bronzes in one building.

Another standout feature of this museum was the range of marble busts, because they were not just done of and for the usual egotistical emperors or nobles. Also included were finely-chiseled impassive children, ordinary people like a butcher with a wart, a blank faced man with a striking resemblance to a middle-aged Leonard Cohen, and on a different wall, as if guarding something, the sobering head and shoulders of a mighty ram.

Having walked through the halls of the museum with their arches that pleasingly mimicked the nearby aqueduct, it would be equally hard to come away without at least a slight impression that the ancient residents of this region had a Dionysian-like love of young boys' bodies (perhaps even to rival that of twenty-first-century feminist writer Germaine Greer.)

The museum closed for lunch. On my way to find somewhere to eat, a street away from my hotel I noticed a man opening up the lid on one of the big green rubbish hoppers that can be found on most Spanish streets. He was pushing a shopping trolley with a few items in it—a couple of strips of twisted metal and some other bits and pieces which I would think of as junk. I had seen many people doing exactly the same since the economic crisis began in 2008. Most were Africans (with or without '*papeles*'—government regis-tration) but more recently it was apparent that not only hard-up migrants were turning to what Americans call dumpster diving.

I told this man (who in 30-plus degree heat was wearing a jumper) that I was a journalist and would pay him three euros for ten minutes of his time if he talked to me. He gave me a sideways glance but shook my hand when I offered it. Noticeably thin and giving off an unpleasantly strong body odour, it has to be said, I asked him what he was doing. Was he collecting something?

"Yes, he said confidently, but with a hint of defensiveness. "I get anything that I can sell and take it to the '*chatarreria*' (scrap yard.) That´s what I do every day. I´ve done it for three hours today and next I´ll go to the other part of town into the industrial area and see what I can find there."

"How long have you been doing this for?"

"Most of my life."

"Do you have a family?"

"I have three kids who go to school and a wife who works a bit."

"And do you have a house?"

"Oh yes. I pay rent. It's controlled by *la junta* (the Extremadura regional government.) And I don't take drugs, y'know. I drink one beer a day and smoke tobacco. That's all." It was only now that he looked me in the eye.

"Okay then. And the people of this town, how are they with you?"

"Fine. Most people ignore me and some offer to buy bread. A few tell me to go and look in other places, but I don't have any trouble. I was born here. I went to school until halfway through secondary school, but now I don't like sitting at home on the sofa. We have to live, right?

I agreed and saw that he was wearing a wristband with the Spanish flag on it so I asked him if he thought Spain is still a good country to live in.

"Of course," he said firmly. "I would never repudiate my home-land. Here, I can work for myself because I don't have a boss."

So this man, who it would be easy to see as a victim of the continuing economic crisis, did not think of himself that way at all. He had the spirit of an independent businessman and believed in action. He found dignity in what he did and his physical energy and drive were keeping him and his family going. When I offered him the money I had promised he declined it, and when I then said that I would buy him some food he told me he didn't need it at the moment. After we shook hands again he went on his way.

In truth, on this trip I was expecting to come across more

people pushing trolleys and scavenging what they could from the objects that we throw away every day. I'd first seen a well-dressed man doing this near our apartment early one morning in the first year of the crisis (in about 2008) and had been disturbed by it. In an article prompted by witnessing these kind of sights, I had recently written:

This so-called crisis, which would more accurately be called a "depression," is a thousand varied things that need never have happened.

Despite the occasional sensation that life is just continuing on very much as before, the crisis here is certainly the more obvious things that many of us see when we care to look: more beggars on the streets, queues in shoe repair shops, the recent appearance of solitary men selling tissues or cigarette lighters on the trains and Metro, a greater number of empty shops for sale or rent (or replaced by cheapo-import Chinese shops) and it is also reading more socio-political graffiti on walls. The crisis is a European-wide failure of institutions like the financial system and the pathetic political response to it, but it is also a very immediate, local phenomenon. In the small town where I live, three years ago there was both a bank and a restaurant—now there is neither.

As well, there are the abstract statistics that simply cannot put a human face to this tragedy - day after day of grim, sullen economic news. A (recent) newspaper headline stated that "60% of Andalusian children live in poverty." This sounds remote and abstract until we learn that there were children in Catalonia who were still going to school in July just to eat lunch, and they had to do this because it is next to impossible for their parents to provide daily meals at home.

But the crisis is about work too. It is hearing that another man has lost his job, or finding that your wife's job has been cut in half and therefore her income has also been halved. It is thousands of workers still lucky enough to have a job but not being "lucky" enough to get paid for their labour...for yet another month. And it is the insult of "mini-jobs" (the underpaid 'mileurista' (who makes 1,000 Euros a month) is seeming like the one who is well-off) or it is listening to people at a café talking about the benefits of learning Chinese or German, ahead of English.

As well, the crisis is the news media being full of corrupt, cowardly politicians talking about everything except what could end the crisis. For thousands of people not in the aptly-termed "political class," it is a rapid or a gradual descent into poverty—what George Orwell called "the crust-wiping,"—that constant search for ways to save money but still ending up unsatisfied after you eat. On top of all this, the crisis is that all-day sensation of being unpleasantly squeezed by the invisible forces of debt, a permanent unconscious burden that is carried by the unemployed and underemployed when a family has no genuine bread-winner.

But what is it that has saved this country from violence, riots and social disturbance on a grand scale? The family. The extended family, acting as helpers, carers and givers of money, love, and as many kinds of assistance that you can think of. Without this blood-linked stability across Mediterranean Europe, things would surely be even worse.

Sometimes, when I have thought about the crisis I have been reminded of a Bob Dylan line about how the sun starts to shine on him. But then (in a single phrase that could speak for millions of Europe's economic victims) he sadly sings "but it's not like the sun that used to be."

❦

THE NEXT DAY, I WAS AGAIN ACROSS MÉRIDA'S RIVER WALKING through the narrow streets behind the bus station. Here were the same cheap, standardised blocks of boxy, mid-twentieth century flats that were in most decent sized towns in Spain. Specifically, these buildings reminded me of high-density *Badia del Vallès* outside Barcelona, across the six-lane highway from the affluent, old-money part of town where I used to teach in a private secondary school. Designed to replicate the shape of Spain on the map and with internal 'immigrants' from places like Mérida and other 'southerners' in mind, it now has the lowest average income of Catalonia, where a third of the population is paid social security allowances. A friend who lives in a nearby town told me that those with problems of long-term, serious drug addiction were sent to live there and today it has a methadone clinic to serve their needs.

But here, opposite these flats in the Extremadura region I was talking to a barman who sold a drug that is more socially accept-able. Over a beer he told me that people like their food "strong" in this part of the country. I had asked him whether I was right about a *tapa* I saw on the covered counter at the bar. Were those really big chunks of raw garlic put on top of sliced tomatoes? He confirmed this and pointed behind the bar to a couple of jars of mini-eggplants pickled in vinegar and paprika that he'd grown on his own farm. I told him I was visiting the area but lived in the Barcelona region.

"Ah, the Catalans think we are lazy," he said, using that word *vaga* again, which can also mean a strike. "They think we don't work and are having parties all the time."

"And do you think that's true?" I asked.

"Well yes, it's a bit true. But we work long hours as well. The Catalans! They are too dull and we are much more open and friendly here."

With regional stereotypes comfortably reinforced, outside on the road I looked across at an ugly, black slab building that was fenced off. This was the town's public library and I thought that I'd never seen such an uninviting library in all my life. At the bus station that was in front of the bar a woman named Fatima sold me a ticket to *Alange* and I sat down to wait. I glanced up and read an unusual announcement crawling across a monitor screen. It said that the platform number for each bus was only 'indicative' and that it was necessary for passengers to listen to the *megáfono* (the PA) because it was possible to "suffer" modifications.

I SPOTTED HER STRAIGHT AWAY IN THE SMALL CROWD AT THE little bus stop. Tall, pale-skinned and with long blonde hair that was greying like mine, Sue looked like she was the only non-Spaniard waiting. I was in the small town of *Alange*, not far from Mérida, and in the strong midday heat we walked through the hilly streets to the *balneario*, the hot springs spa, a world heritage site.

"This is a really lovely place," Sue said. "I get in for free because I do some translating work for them."

She sauntered confidently into the black and white marble entrance hall, with me a step or two behind. I could tell she'd been here many times before. I made noises about getting into the medicinal mineral water, but Sue had already decided that today was not the day for that. She gave me a little tour of the public areas. We passed through to a garden and before I knew it I was outside looking back at the lovely, yolk-coloured four-star hotel that houses the spa. We were out and heading down the road to a bar.

I was disappointed because the place looked like one of my favourite types of relaxation. But I didn't complain, though I could have done with a wallow in the same spring water as the Romans did over two thousand years earlier. Instead I had a beer and listened to Sue tell me about it.

"Of course the work I did for them was unpaid," she said. "I do the same for the town council—classes or translation—and we agree that I have a kind of credit with them that I can use any time. That way I don't have to pay any taxes and we're out of the bureaucratic trap here. Phil (her husband) and I do that back in England, where we have a flat that we rent."

I wanted to know the same thing a lot of people ask me. "How did you come to be here, where there are so few English expats?"

"Well, we'd visited Mérida in Mexico years ago and when we saw the same name on the Spanish map we thought it'd be worth paying a visit to see what it was like. We loved how beautiful it is here and the house was relatively cheap, so we snapped it up. I'm very active in the community in the town. I learnt to speak the language and everyone knows me."

Sue offered to drive me to her house a few kilometres away. As we walked to her car she pointed out some very attractive houses and a couple of well-decorated public buildings. In this hinterland town of less than two thousand people, half a dozen hotels are operating, she said.

Sue drove us past a massive lake. "It's man-made, you know. It was all just open fields, but now people go water skiing here, they fish for carp, they swim or have barbeques on the shores." As far I could see the lake was deserted and would be until the evening, she said.

At Sue's house she introduced me to Phil, her husband, who worked in the IT industry and sometimes commuted back to England to do short-term contracted jobs there. I also met Chemical Alan, their shy greyhound, who was lying like a sphinx across their bed and eyeballed me suspiciously as I walked slowly past the bedroom. From the shade of the front balcony where we had a drink, as they habitually did, was a sweeping view of the lake we had just passed, a little island in the middle of it, as well as a tit-shaped mountain that dominated on one side.

"I've been trying to tell them about tourism and publicising the different events there are, but they haven't got a clue," Phil said. "When hardly anyone turns up they say 'Yes, we told everyone, we invited everybody,' but there's no thought of trying to get people to visit from outside the area."

Sue pointed down to their garden area. "We're trying to be semi-self-sufficient. We barter a bit with the neighbours, swapping whatever we have plenty of with whatever they have a glut of too. More people are doing this kind of thing recently because of 'the crisis.'"

"Yeah, we get by alright," Phil chimed in. "The phone coverage is a bit in and out and that can make it tricky at times, but we like it here." They seemed to me like almost pioneers. After a second drink, Sue drove me back to the bus station in Mérida. On the way she told me how she spent some of her time doing occasional blogging, on top of proofreading and editing manuscripts.

"The only thing I really hate is travel writing," she said, staring down the road.

Back in Mérida that night, in crowded *Plaza de España* square, I drank a takeaway '*granizado*'—a crushed ice fruit drink popular in the summer months. This one was not the usual lemon kind, but was a *sangria* version made with red wine and rum. I'd never seen this before (or since) and I kept the hard plastic beaker it came in as a souvenir. As I sipped it, sitting on steps at the side of the square because all the benches were taken, I watched the crowd. This was such a fundamental part of life in this country: public life, life open to the elements, life open to chance encounters. It was a social setting that did not demand paying for anything or consuming something except the free night air. Unlike the average outdoor gathering in the USA, Australia or Britain there was no monetary imperative.

As was so common in Spain, people of every age were out tonight—children playing football near me using some bushes as goals, old woman in floral skirts standing in pairs or trios gesticulating together, couples with babies, and old men silently smoking. Spread around a few of the corners of the square were clutches of teenagers. They were looking for action.

It was this quintessential scene that always told me I was somewhere else, vastly different from my suburban Australian childhood with its commerce-first shopping mall, bicycle paths and backyard sport. Twenty years ago, while spending three months travelling across Europe (but firstly in Paris) I had discovered a kind of casual recreation in public parks and squares that I never knew existed. In Canberra, where I grew up, the park was generally for drunks or had a half-broken set of swings or maybe a rusty old slide for little kids. That was all. But as a traveller 'on the continent' and then living in Spain I had come to love people-watching in public places like these: my partner Paula had shown me how and why to do it. I'd learnt that plenty of people spent time in parks only partly because most European city dwellers live in smallish apartments with just a cramped balcony or terrace for fresh air. The park or square can be a social place, of course, but is also for solitude, though usually amongst others.

Ignoring the "Burguer Buggy," (sic) my hunger tonight took me to a busy tapas bar on one edge of the square specialising in Spanish ham. (I later found out that the long pedestrian shopping street it was on is called *Calle John Lennon*, a boyhood hero of mine.) At the bar I was tired, and without thinking, asked for a plate of *serrano* ham—as I usually did back in *Catalunya*. This request set off great laughter with a couple of the waiters. "Sure," one of them chuckled, "I can get you some of *that*. We could even serve *serrano* here!"

Behind me, a man who I had heard speaking Catalan to his wife made a joke that I didn't catch and guffawed with the bartender/waiter. I said good evening to him in Catalan, which produced a surprised expression on his face. Then I tried to correct my culinary blunder with the staff. Naturally, this was the kind of establishment that looked down on anything except the pricier, richer-flavoured *Iberico* ham as being cheap and nasty—certainly inferior. In short, their attitude was that *serrano* ham was unfit to be served here, but the joke was that they'd send someone into a late night supermarket to scrounge up a few dried-out slices of it, if that's what some ignorant tourist wanted.

In reality, it's not easy to overstate the importance of the pig and pork products to Spain and its people. In harsher centuries it had even been used as a weapon of ethnic cleansing when suspected closet-Muslims were forced to eat it to prove they had in fact converted to Catholicism. On average today, a Spanish adult eats a total of five kilos a year of ham alone—one huge whole leg each.

In fact, the *Iberico* ham that I realised I should have been ordering is surely one of the world's greatest, most unique artisan foods. Production is very strictly regulated, and the free-range black-footed *pata negra* pigs that it comes from eat mainly acorns that fall straight off the trees. This makes the final product naturally high in omega-3 oil, lending it a succulent, sweet, nutty-flavoured fat that can still be tasted on the tongue minutes after it's eaten. Real *jamon iberico* produces an aroma that is one of the truly evocative smells of Spain. When you walk past one of the specialist ham shops or delis that are even in many smallish towns and get a whiff of this delicacy, you know you are not in Sydney, Tokyo or Bristol.

Being in Extremadura, I had considered visiting one of the *jamon iberico* pig farms that are common to the area but Sue Sharpe had advised me against it. She told me before I arrived, "I don't know of any *pata negra* farms that haven't been 'Disneyfied,' for want of a better term. There are tour companies that can organise an 'experience,' but they don't normally operate in the heat of an Extremadura summer."

Still though, waiters and bartenders might have to get used to some other odd requests from visitors. I later read online that in December of this year film director Woody Allen and his New Orleans Jazz Band would be doing a concert in the nearby town of Badajoz "with other, smaller performances that may follow in the land-locked region's other two main cities, Mérida and *Cáceres*."

Over at the town's train station the next morning I tried to get information about RENFE trains leaving the next day. I spoke to a man of about sixty years of age behind the only ticket desk. His short-sleeved shirt was open halfway down his stomach and he couldn't give me a train timetable. There was apparently no map of where the lines went. All the fragments of times and places he told verbally and when I asked him to write them down he tore a small, rough piece of paper from a pad and scribbled on it. All the trains apparently went to small towns in the area or back to Madrid— there was nothing going south to Seville or Córdoba where I wanted to head. So, it would have to be the bus for me. On the way out I noticed there were no ticket machines in this quiet little cool station. I laughed. Behind me was a little girl marching up and down chanting "I shit in the milk! I shit in the milk." I knew how she felt.

❧ 3 ❧

CÓRDOBA

Sometimes the earth's surface repeats itself. What you see from a bus window going from Mérida to Seville and then on to Córdoba is virtually the same as the 800 kilometres from Sydney to Melbourne on the Hume highway, with the exception of Australia's sheep. (Even just the words 'Hume Highway' evoke an instant historical ache of tedium in my guts.) In January in the winter of 1997 I'd done this same bus ride to Seville and remembered it similarly. About travelling through this part of Spain this time around, in my notebook I wrote in a shaky hand:

"*I am not the man to comment on or describe what I am seeing. It holds no interest for me because I have lived these simple scenes for many, many hours in my earlier life.*"

I chose instead to read my book and view the highly personal inner landscape of Goytisolo through his creamy prose and sharp dissection of the "ill-formed universe" of his bourgeois upbringing. In *Forbidden Territory*, he at times speaks to himself in the second person and uses italics, saying in a revealing part:

"*To the extent that your attachment to your mother vanished with her, you can say quite truthfully that rather than her son, the son of a woman who is and will always be unknown to you, you are a son of the civil war,*

its Messianism, cruelty, and anger: of the unhappy accumulation of circum-
stances that brought into the open the real entrails of the country and filled
you with a youthful desire to abandon it forever..."

Goytisolo later goes onto say: "The day I finally broke loose, I
already lived outside mentally. When you go away it is because you
have already left." I had felt exactly the same when I had originally
left Australia and my mind too was on a destination ahead.
Momentarily abandoning the traveller's code of living in the
moment, I calculated that I was about as far away from Goytisolo's
birthplace and my adopted home as I could be, while still being in
the same country.

Unbeknown to me at that time, I was now passing through the
flatlands and low hills where from the mid-1950s a nine-year-old
boy had started a dozen years of living with wolves. Marcos
Rodríguez Pantoja says that not long after his mother died and his
family was living in a stick hut, his father (who was a charcoal
maker and a violent man) "sold him like a pig" to a local farmer.
When this farmer died Pantoja was alone and went into the
wilderness. He says that he would howl and the wolves would
come to him. He would eat with them and sometimes sleep with
them for warmth, accepted because he had their smell. Not
wanting to return to the human world that he felt was much
crueler than the wild, he found that animals could be his friends
and those he didn't hunt with his knife he learnt methods of
survival from. Pantoja became an expert in bird calls and other
animal noises. When, as an adult, he was eventually found by
police, he was locked up for a few days. Then he was sent to live
with nuns, where he would only sleep under his bed, never in it.
His remarkable story was subsequently verified by anthropologists
who studied him and was the model for the 2010 film titled *Among*
Wolves.

I WAS WAITING IN SEVILLE'S BUS STATION LOOKING OUT ONTO

the Guadalquivir River, but I was anticipating a comfortable bed in Córdoba. It was my third visit to Seville. I'd liked it before but found it a bit too much of a big city and too touristy for my liking to stay there again.

Córdoba, however, is like Seville's aunty or Granada's cousin to me. Unlike almost all standard tourist towns, it doesn't possess more than one major attraction, and that is one thing that appeals to me about it: Córdoba is usually bypassed on the main package holiday routes. It also doesn't have the same quality of public transport connections as many other Spanish cities and month after month of fierce heat puts many people off visiting the city, especially since there is no beach within easy reach (as both Seville and Granada have.) With perverse pride, it proclaims itself as being the hottest provincial capital in Spain since1991.

Somewhat worryingly, the day I arrived on a bus the city's main newspaper was reporting a bus crash in nearby Toledo province. Fifty people had been injured. Also commented on in the paper was apparent "new life" for Pablo Iglesias, leader of the anti-austerity party *Podemos*. For probably the first time, a poll was putting him in clear third place behind the two parties who had taken turns governing the country since the restart of democratic elections a generation ago. Related to this was another story about how the level of unemployment had again risen to the same point as it had been in 2011, when Rajoy's conservatives had won office. A few pages away from reports of life and death at the local bull-fights, I noted an article about a forty-year-old woman who had been found slain in her home: apparently a victim of domestic violence. In this country it is simply called *machista* (or 'male chau-vinist') violence. The reporter observed that there had been another four cases of this same crime during the previous four days.

Much less tragically, what Córdoba also has is plenty of authen-ticity as an example of Andalucía at its best. The city is dotted with lovely, shady gardens—many with fountains—and has some-thing I always value in a town or city: it has 'walkability.' In other words, for a visitor, no place you'd want to see or do something at is too far from anywhere else significant and can be easily reached on foot.

I stayed at a cheap hotel next to the bus station. This bus station, which I discovered has an astonishing three cafés and a pleasant little circular garden of ferns and tall trees in the middle —is also right next to the train station. The train station is only a twenty-minute walk from the historic centre: a rare stroke of Spanish planning (which is virtually an oxymoron anyway). This combined proximity alone creates a degree of pleasure, since a true feel for a city cannot be gained from, say, getting on an underground train and popping up here or there on the map (as I did to my great confusion and detriment in London the first time) .

One morning my feet took me down the long *Avenida de la República Argentina*, and then near the bullring, I cut up *Camino de los Sastres*, named after the small street that had once been for tailors' workshops. It was only 9.30, but already a couple of pink-skinned tourists were seeking the shade while walking, as I was, behind the imposing *Alcazar* castle. It was here where Ferdinand II and Isabella spent most of their royal lives, setting up the horrors of the Spanish Inquisition and ordering the expulsion or forced conversion of the country's Jews and Muslims.

At one of the gates to the ancient city, the *Puerta Almodóvar*, I found *La Judería*, the old Jewish quarter. Here again were the narrow alleys that I always love so much—a few of them so narrow that you had to turn sideways to allow another person to walk past you. While Europe's massive churches and cathedrals tend to make you feel small and remind you of the truth of our existential insignificance, these tight spaces have the opposite effect—they turn the psyche inward on itself and, to me, can encourage the kind of internal dialogue that leads to creative impulses. The wanderer gets physically lost, just as getting lost in thought can produce originality in, say, music, poetry or even philosophy.

Spain has only recently started to discover the power of the Semitic tourist, and souvenir shops were now not only catering to them but to Muslims as well. Córdoba was no different, but the old town was not crowded with hunters of keyrings and plates. In fact business looked very slow. I was able to enjoy a convivial haggle with a jewelry shop owner and bought a couple of well-priced pieces for my wife's upcoming birthday.

At the basic hotel where I was staying, when I asked for a map I'd been given one that had marked on it all of the thirty bars and restaurants that had competed in the First Annual Tapas Competition during November 2012. This encouraged me but I hardly needed or used the map.

At lunchtime today I ate early like a tourist, for a change. I sat with no other diners at a *taberna* in the La Ribera, an area that overlooks the river—the same baby-shit brown Guadalquivir that flows through the middle of Seville. One expat blogger goes as far as to say that she believes that the view from the top of the nearby *mezquita* over this river is one of the best in Spain, but at this moment my eyes were on the menu. I happily consumed a good piece of flaky salt-cod, but the strong co-op white wine was not cold and the service was slow. I satisfied myself with the view along the street next to the new *Miraflores* Bridge. When a gypsy man pushed a cart along the curb, I said to myself that I could have been watching him in the nineteenth century.

While eating, I also read a local paper. I learnt that Córdoba was running its first (500-word) short story competition on the theme of public transport. First prize was a tablet and one hundred euros worth of free transport in the city.

But my transport today was my feet. Walking through the old town on this summer afternoon there was no evidence of the kind of poverty that Hispanist Gerald Brenan had witnessed a generation ago. It was a clear sign of both the nation's and Córdoba's economic progress—from what was popularly called '*los años de desarrollo*' (the development years after 1960) that a visitor would no longer see, as Brennan had, "children of ten with wizened faces, women of thirty who are already hags (and) lepers that look (more) wretched than those of Marrakesh and Taroudant."

Later that night, I passed through a public garden that was displaying hundreds of small multi-coloured flags. They were part of a protest against the Israeli government's military action in Gaza and were accompanied by a prominent list of the names of those who had been killed. I was heartened to see that in a provincial city like this one there were people who were well aware of events a long way outside their own area. The continuing existence of this display in a public place was an example of local government tolerance towards left-wing causes, and I wondered if the same attitude would be shown by the town hall in conservative Madrid, 400 kilometres away.

Then I was in a different park around fountains once more, a reminder to me of the Moor's love of water. Looking away from the locals who were enjoying the now cooler air, I stood alongside the *Avenida de la Libertad* (Freedom Avenue), which changes its name to the Avenida Al-Nasir on one of its sides and *Avenida de los Piconeros* (coal makers) then *Avenida de Igualdad* (equality) on the other side. Typical of the European mania for it in many Spanish towns, I guessed that these names were changed after Franco's dictatorship: the abstract nature of their new titles suggests an attempt at ideological renewal.

Even in the little village where I live, the street had been called General Mola—one of Franco's co-plotters in his coup—until the end of the 1970s, when it was changed back to Ángel Guimerá, after the Catalan language writer. I had a Catalan friend, a psychologist with a Jewish grandmother, who would take this concept even further. He would regularly go out at night in his city of Terrassa, sometimes as part of a determined little group, and pull down any signs or symbols that had any connection with General Franco.

This long Córdoba avenue that disappeared into the night horizon made me recall the kind of heavy-handed street planning I'd seen in East Berlin. Lovely orange trees lining its flanks were not enough to persuade me that through the dark distance at the avenue's end there would not be a square with some hideous totalitarian statue or monument plonked in it. Where this main road begins beside the train station, by chance earlier in the day I'd come across some archaeological digs on the more than two-millennia-old Via Augusta. The "longest Roman road anywhere in Hispania, (it covers) some 1,500 kilometres from the Pyrenees Mountains, skirting the Mediterranean Sea as far as Cadiz" on the Atlantic south-west peninsula.

Here was a comparison of sorts: an empire of antiquity versus mid-twentieth-century totalitarian angles. If you see a long straight road between towns in Britain or continental Europe you can generally assume it has a Roman origin, like the stretch of the Via Augusta past the Catalan town where I lived. On the other hand, if you see a long straight boulevard in a city there is a good chance that it's the hand of a modern megalomaniac behind it.

In the wider scope of history, Córdoba was once a great centre of three cultures: Muslim, Christian and Jewish. The city even passed through long periods where these three religions coexisted simultaneously in relative harmony. Now, Córdoba was at the centre of two unholy rows—one over the name of its only famous landmark, *la mezquita*, and the other a semi-related spat about, not sacred wine, but beer.

A thousand years ago the ancient town had over three hundred mosques, so it seems reasonable that at least one of these should still stand with the name 'mosque' or *mezquita* in Castilian Spanish. The *mezquita* is the only big drawcard for visitors, being a UNESCO Cultural Heritage Site and Spain's most important Islamic building. When I first entered it back in 1997, I had been bowled over by the forest of painted red and white striped arches inside. It had the effect of placing me in a kind of wonderland.

But an agency of the Catholic Church has recently made every possible attempt to eliminate the name *'mezquita'* from the building, which has long been a cathedral. In a cynical exercise, by stealth they have tried to change its title, first to the Mosque-Cathedral, then simply the Cathedral of Córdoba—now used in all church publications. At the very same time they have been hypocritically registering virtually every conceivable variation on the words '*Mezquita*' and '*Catedral*' in twenty-five different categories of brand trademarking.

Several months after my trip, back in a Catalonia supermarket I bought a four-pack of *Mezquita* beer, made in Córdoba, celebrating the thousand-year reign. This seemed inaccurate to me. 1013 was the same year that Spain was "separated into small kingdoms," but glorifying this ignored the fact that the Muslim Moors were controlling much of the country, including the jewel of Toledo in that same year. I liked the beer though. The label said that "after a long repose in the cellar, its attributes are rounded, creating an intense, firm body." After a few bottles I certainly fancied a repose for my rounded body (that is anything except firm), but thought little more about it until late the following winter when news articles started to appear about this beer.

It turned out that the Catholic Church organisation in charge of its many and varied Spanish business interests had registered a new beer named '*Mezquita Catedral*.' The problem was that the beer I'd enjoyed was already on the market, using the word *Mezquita* as its name. As reported, "Mahou, the owner of the *Mezquita* brand through its *Cervezas Alhambra* unit, fought the Catholic Church's attempt to register a similar trademark. They appealed to the Patent Office on the grounds that consumers may get confused by the similarity of both brand names," but were rejected. It was only the Madrid Regional High Court's later ruling that came down in the company's favour, declaring that the church could not use the word *Mezquita* in any alcoholic drinks it manufactures or owns.

I walked to the *Mezquita*. Then I walked away from the *Mezquita*. They wanted to charge eight euros entry fee. I had already signed a petition to keep its name and had no desire to fund any of the church's activities. Anyway, it was part of my policy on this trip to be as cultural as possible at the lowest cost and I had great memories of the *Mezquita's* interior. I knew if I went in again I would be debasing those memories because I would be grinding my teeth, partly due to the cost of entry.

The other pleasing recollection that had stayed with me from that time was a visit to the museum dedicated to the Cordovan artist, Julio Romero de Torres. His paintings of smoldering, long-legged beauties with dark hair and dark eyes (many of them semi-naked) reflected the women I saw in the streets. It was my first week in Spain and my thoughts ran wildly. I'd had other reasons to be excited as well. On the quiet night bus to Granada out of the awful overdeveloped Costa del Sol, a trio of girls in their late teens across the aisle from me stripped and changed clothes, giggling all the while and casting looks in my direction. My then girlfriend Paula slept silently in the seat next to me and we'd been in Spain for only a couple of hours. I sat wondering what kind of land of milk and honey I had arrived at.

৩ﾒﾓ

A FRIEND OF MINE NAMED RAÚL BLANCO HAS A FATHER WHO originally came from Córdoba.

He told me that when his father, called Sixto (probably after one of the Popes) was seventeen he decided to try his luck finding work in Barcelona. Like a lot of the Spaniards at that time he was regularly living on little food—the 1940s and '50s were often called 'the years of hunger'—and he was prepared to risk what was then an illegal train trip due to the tight restrictions on travelling away from your hometown.

Sixto was told by his friends to stand in the open space between the two carriages of the train and when it started to slow down before Barcelona, around the town of Sitges on the *Garraf* coast he should then jump off onto the ground. He was warned to do this only when he heard the announcement for the stop at Sitges.

But Sixto did not hear the pronunciation of the town with a hard 'g' sound that he was accustomed to. Instead the soft "ch" of

'Seetchas' in the Catalan accent was used and when he soon arrived in Barcelona and got off the train that was supposed to take him to a bright new future he was arrested on the platform, thrown into jail for nine days, then sent back to Córdoba.

Sixto was not deterred for long though. The next time he made sure that through his family he had arranged a work contract with former neighbours who had agreed to officially sponsor him and his employment in Barcelona. One of his first jobs was being a labourer on the *Camp Nou*, a new stadium for the city's beloved *Barça* football team. Like many of his fellow so-called 'immigrants' he lived in the working class area of *Hospitalet de Llobregat* where, with his wife (from the northern Burgos region), he went on to run a bar-restaurant.

Sixto's story is emblematic and typical of his generation of rural families, especially those from Andalucía, a region where the Socialist party has governed without losing office since 1982. His hometown of Córdoba was actually the first provincial capital to elect a Communist mayor. In King Solomon's time Andalucía was called *'Tarshish'* in Hebrew. (The biblical character Jonah was sailing there until he was swallowed by 'the great fish.') *Tarshish* was then considered to be the legendary place of riches at the end of the world, but if Sixto had known about this before he stepped onto the train he might have thought of it as a cruel joke.

I HAD THE TIME AND FREEDOM AFFORDED TO AN INDEPENDENT traveller, so I got on a bus. Just to be perverse, I wanted to go to the hottest part of the country in the hottest part of the month at the hottest time of the day. I made the decision to arrive in *Écija,* the town known to Spaniards as *"La sartén"* (the frying pan) because it records the nation's highest temperatures, at around two o'clock, half hoping and half expecting that it would be near deserted—a kind of ghost town sauna.

On the bus trip there I talked to two Koreans. As a joke, I had started by asking one of them if he wanted a souvenir and then showed him my seat belt buckle. It was broken and not even attached to the seat. They were both engineers working for Hyundai and were involved in shipbuilding. On holiday, their plan was to see some bullfighting and go to Barcelona Football club next week. "Is gambling on football illegal here?" one of them asked. He had been told that it was not a good idea to talk politics with Spanish people and admitted to not knowing much about the country. He could tell me with a surprising degree of certainty, though, that he didn't like China: it was too noisy and dirty and its people were too proud of Chinese culture, in his opinion.

When I stepped off the bus at *Écija* the first sensation was like feeling an electric hair dryer blowing softly into my face. Soon after, as I walked towards the centre of town, the tips of my ears seemed to be burning, though it was only 41 degrees. Standing on one of the main streets at a bar window I talked to a Romanian barman. "Every day is more difficult," he said plaintively, and I thought of Bob Dylan's beautiful song about pitying the immigrant.

I too was an immigrant—a long-term one—but this man wanted to get to England or even Australia, he told me. Behind him on the walls inside the bar were fascist-looking crossed flags and posters of bullfights. Two fat middle-aged men were glaring aggressively at me, both smoking cigarettes at stools indoors—completely against the law and a very rare sight nowadays.

Twenty metres away was the town's main square, *Plaza de España*: a large rectangle with porticoed colonnades covering one side. The tourist office on the other side was closed (summer, afternoon!) and I could see a modern underground carpark set at the far end. I later found out that this recent construction had been at the cost of what an archaeologist called "one of the great cities of the Roman world," a place almost as important in the Roman world as Córdoba and Seville. Only discovered in 1998, the then mayor Juan Wic had been keen to deliver on his election promise to increase municipal car parking in the centre of town.

Most of this lost city is known as Colonia Augusta Firma Astigi and its 2,000-year-old "well-preserved Roman forum, bath house, gymnasium and temple as well as dozens of private homes and hundreds of mosaics and statues" were simply concreted over to make spaces for two hundred and ninety cars.

At the moment there seemed little else to do today so, for the first time in a very long time I ambled into a church just off the main square. This one had the appearance of that colonial style that brought to mind South American prayer houses. After all, many of that continent's conquerors had come from the wider area —Aztec slayer *Hernán* (or Hernando) Cortés (to give just one example) was born in 1485 in Extremadura's *Medellín*. Inside it was musty smelling, and amongst many others, there was a painting of Jesus in a white frock crying black tears against his pale face. I sat in the courtyard making notes under a '*matraca de la torre*'—a giant wooden cross, probably for carrying by penitents on holy days. A collection of small art items with the label "possibly taken from Costa Rica or Colombia" had been gathered for display in front of some offices.

On a street named *Calle Cinteria* I walked in the comforting shade of blue and white striped canvas awnings high overhead— the kind that had been used for at least a century to cover these narrow alleys. The effect was calming. It could have been the influence of the strong sun, but it seemed to me that there was more than the usual number of ice cream shops scattered through the centre. As well, I saw a couple of shops specialising in organic olive oil and noted this as a sign of progress, away from the strictly traditional. I asked a local woman for directions, then inquired about what she likes to eat in the summer. Apart from salad and drinking beer she recommended *salmorejo*—tomato and bread soup, thicker than its famous cousin, *gazpacho*.

In a bakery I asked the woman serving about a round loaf of bread that had the shape of a pterodactyl dinosaur. I hadn't seen anything made in that shape before. She picked it up and showed it to me, proudly telling me that it was a regional specialty and more crunchy on the outside than normal bread. These two women had been friendly and helpful. It all made me sad to see a public notice nearby that advised that thirty-three local women had died as a result of domestic violence so far this year. And it was only August.

Back near the bus station I came across the town bullring. A poster advertised that spunky, hunky Barcelona-born flamenco singer Miguel Poveda had played there the previous week. Smack bang in the middle of the main street that leads in and out of town was a statue of an older, heroic Miguel, this one of *Don Quixote* author Cervantes. I thought it was an odd work of art. A sharp-angled, metallic Cervantes had been depicted reading a book, while underneath him, inside an even bigger book, other figures (seemingly arguing) were struggling to hold up, or possibly open or close their book. What could that all mean? The inscription referred to *Écija* as "sun city"—something I could not have argued with.

Then, across the road, I followed a man into a building through an unmarked door, intrigued by the all-red, painted-out glass windows of what I took to be some kind of bar. There were no words or sign on the outside, only the letters 'RS' in large font. When I ordered a beer I asked the barman what this place was. A club of some kind?

"No, this is a casino."

"So, how's business?" I inquired.

"It's not as busy as it used to be."

"What kind of people come here?"

"Well, ninety-nine percent of our clients are men."

"Do you get any Chinese people coming in?"

"Yeah we do. But in Spain it gets very hot in August and people don't come in so much. It gets up near fifty degrees and you can fry an egg outside," he said with a distinct lack of originality.

"Who owns this place, then?"

"Ah well, my boss is a private man but I can tell you that he owns another six casinos across this country."

There was some historical precedent for this successful business. According to Miguel de Unamuno, an independent-minded pre-Civil War Spanish writer and philosopher, gambling was the "terrible scourge of the Extremadurans" who neighboured this area. He also believed that this problem could explain the adventurous spirit of the conquerors of South America.

But just ten kilometres away from *Écija*, the profit motive of any casino owner or other business-person is now almost a thing of the past in the town of *Marinaleda*. It had been described as a Utopian Socialist democracy, and a participatory democracy at that. Long known for the quality of its olives and oil, *Marinaleda* was attracting media attention over the town's unconventional Mayor, Juan Manuel Sánchez Gordillo, who'd earned the nickname, 'The Spanish Robin Hood.'

He had led groups of local people in what he called "non-violent acts of disobedience" where they broke into supermarkets (while they were open and staffed during the day) and took basic food items to supply a local food bank. In the wider province there are almost 700,000 empty properties—many because of bank repossessions—but according to journalist Sophie McAdam this is not the case in *Marinaleda*. "Mayor Gordillo has a solution: anyone who wants to build their own house can do so for free. Materials and qualified workmen are provided by the town hall, and the generous allowance of 192 square metres means the homes are spacious. Families then pay just 15 euros ($19) per month for the rest of their lives, with the agreement that the house cannot be sold for private gain."

All in all, I concluded that *Marinaleda* might be a good town to live in and if I'd been travelling around by car I certainly would have paid it a visit. I was relying solely on public transport and instead got on the bus back to Córdoba. This time I decided to examine the landscape outside the window. In one place patches of sunflowers looked like they had been blowtorched. In another vista the land had the wrinkly appearance of a badly ironed shirt. Further on there were sand-coloured dune-like hills and the spiky texture of their plants reminded me of my childhood stickle brick toys with their pleasing, bumpy rows. These were Andalucía's olive trees—the main crop and a source of employment that was still holding on despite the economic crisis.

It astounded me that anything would grow and prosper in this harsh climate, but I am a city boy and cannot grow a plant to save myself. Not quite as common as the olive trees, but just as striking, were the demented clumps of cactuses I saw huddling together. They were the size of fully grown humans. The British author and long-time Málaga resident Robert Graves had once taunted George Moore (another writer) with having introduced cactus into one of his Holy Land stories some fifteen centuries before the discovery of America, the cactus' land of origin.

Not far from the roadside was a different kind of taunt. A large golden Moorish dome on top of a furniture shop was being silently mocked by dozens and dozens of seemingly empty new apartments: plenty of sofas and no customers. Next came the pink "*Scandolo* Club" (i.e., brothel), but I was grabbed instead by a great lusty panorama: a sea of green sand hills that stretched off to the horizon. This was beauty unbesmirched by a single road or building or fence and the lines of olive trees across it were like the scrapes of a fork through a mound of mashed potato: easily the equal of Tuscany's most picturesque scenes.

Back at the hotel on TV, a supposed expert was talking in serious tones about the two opposite extremes of '*tanophobia* and *tanorexia*'—fear of getting a tan as opposed to tan addiction. These were completely new concepts to me. The TV expert advised viewers to "take neither too much nor too little sun." There seemed to be a fine line between some public health warnings and being patronised.

❧ 4 ❧

INTERLUDE: AS IT IS, AS IT WAS—
ASTURIAS

I remember—when I must have been no more than ten years old—somehow hearing the Australian classical guitarist John Williams play a flamenco-influenced piece called "Asturias." For me then, as now, it was the exotic, the other. I'd never heard anything like it and I remember being transfixed. More than anything else this piece of music still brings to mind the sensation of movement, but also the shape of a spiral in the mind. It features a repeated, incessant rhythm that is something like a noise running through a tunnel. It had been composed by Isaac Albéniz, a Catalan-born child prodigy. For more than four years I worked in a school in a street named after him, in Vallpineda, an upper part of Sitges. Albéniz believed himself to have been from Jewish descent, once writing, "I was named Isaac, in honor of the Jews who undulated into Spain from the East, embracing (the) Holy Church to avoid the rigors of the rack during the Inquisition."

Not too long ago, along with several other expat writers, I was invited by the regional Tourism Board of Asturias to visit and stay in one of the Parador hotels in the capital city, Gijon. We were flown there, fed wonderful local food and wine and then taken separately by local guides around different parts of Asturias. The only expectation was that we would write about our experiences.

Quite simply, I was astonished with what I found over the next four days. I had lived in Spain for many years, but barely knew anything about Asturias. I soon learnt how uninformed I had been.

჻

ASTURIAN COAL MINER: A PORTRAIT

The coal miner's wife wakes him and he coughs. He shuffles to the small bathroom sink and spits black liquid, washing it away with the brown tap water.

Last night he slept badly, suffering from stomach cramps, diarrhea and vomiting again. He had been working in the zinc mine at *Arnao in Castrillon,* but the Belgian company who own the site have let him go to the San Juan mine. He felt himself to be quite lucky. At least there they had a river pool for the miners to wash in.

As he leaves for another day under the earth, the miner looks for a last time at the mountains, at their ferns and the tall groups of eucalyptus—pencil thin, not quite straight, just like the trees in a Doctor Seuss book. He sees the houses with their sharp pitched roofs in front of deep gorges and is comforted by the roll of the hills across this green land.

Our miner is living before the era of the chemical plants and big metal factories. He knows others who dig for iron and knows it's vital for tinned food because electricity and refrigeration have not yet arrived to this part of the world.

His mine, like many mines, is close to a river: a means of transporting the coal for trading this raw material with British towns like Cardiff and Newcastle-upon-Tyne (where my own father was born and also grew up next to a polluted river).

This miner's children will one day see the construction of chemical industries, thanks to the mines, thanks to his labour. In fact, he thinks, as he makes the walk to the pits, the story of

Asturias is the story of the miner and the story of the miner is the story of Asturias. It is one of hardship and scant reward, of growth but also ill health. It is a tale of the deep earth's hidden secrets and humanity's immeasurable suffering with the open spaces of the valleys and their claustrophobic confines—as unforgiving and back-breaking as any imagined hell in those greedy shafts penetrating ever downwards into the planet.

Today, like thousands of other days, he will launch his body into the ground and probe hour after hour for that black rock. Finally, at the end of the day our miner will take aspirin for his aching bones, smiling at the ironic fact that it has ingredients made from the very coal he has been digging for. He does not yet know, though, that decades later, his children are going to eat kiwi-fruits and chestnuts that will come to grow particularly well in the carbon-coloured soil left from abandoned open-cut mines scattered across the nearby hills.

As the miner eats his simple lunch with his hands still blackened by coal dust, he remembers his father, who was also a miner. He too worked to extract the iron that was in such high demand for both twentieth-century world wars—a metal that helped the rich become richer. His father started life as a rural worker and had to adapt from the rhythms of the seasons to the very different rhythm of an industrial timetable. He had to learn to accept days and nights with no sky or trees, down in the mines which lay right next to his cramped terrace house.

Like every other subterranean labourer, his father and he both wondered if life could ever be different for them. He'd heard that things were a bit better at the only mine run by a trade union. But it was on the other side of Asturias and he had never even visited there.

Our miner lives in *Bustiello* town where all of the aristocrat Marques de Camilla's workers have their neat little houses below everyone else, at the bottom of the valley. It is an orderly, rectangular village, and each house has a small garden. Up the hill above them live the engineers and above them is the church, then

God of course. This is what he knows: the planning of the town exactly reflects the social and spiritual hierarchy. The Marques is a conservative man. He fears the progressive men who want social change.

Further on in the mountains there are mining zones that suffered from "special measures" during Franco's dictatorship. Around *Pozo Fortuna* ('the lucky well') trade union activists were assassinated and their bodies were thrown down an old pit-hole. Our miner speaks about this sadly with his friends and later falls asleep hoping that the bad times will end.

In the morning, he rises and faces another day.

The Colors of Asturias—a poem

if we must have any damn flags at all
the flag of the region
should be green
black
and red

Asturias is certainly verdant green
but it is also
black

the black of the miner's lung
and the almost permanent colour of his stained spit
it is also that sightless place of no mercy
at the bottom of the pit where
another of Franco's victims is thrown
this region has a history the colour of carbon
the same earthy tint as morcilla blood sausage
those guts and organs that have fed its people
and black like

the hide of a cow
who has quietly ruminated
on its producing hills

and there is that ash black of a thousand widow's dresses
mixed with the black of children's despair
at their father's early death
the same dim sackcloth shade
of the early morning forest where
the dictator's enemies hid shivering
hungry but unbroken

and the crucial Asturian black
the lump of its fresh coal now released
or a neglected fully-rotten pear
slate like the night-time ocean that empties itself
into rivers like the Nalón
as brutal as an unlit mine

and this colour too might have been
the charcoal feathers of a bird
that flew over and coldly watched
all this great grim past
with its darting granite eyes

also austere Asturias has a culture
full of red
red like trees of ripened apples
that make the drinker's everyday cider
but not as red
as those huge painted silos that hold it all

the enflamed red too of the wildflowers that grow here
and the smoky paprika powder that is sprinkled
on boiled potatoes

again and again

but it is also the red of the dead
the civil war corpses and the slaughtered soldiers
that vile hue that inhabits the church wine
though also the *vino tinto* waiting on the table

or there is even that red
like the double bars of the Spanish flag
with that saffron yellow lying
in between those rusty stripes

and functioning like a tale
that arterial red
of painted iron trains
the *ferrocarril*
that opened up the heart
of this day's Asturias.

❦ 5 ❦

TO FRIGILIANA

I would have preferred the train to Málaga but it was more than double the price of the bus. The train takes about half the time of the bus but I was in no big hurry. I had the luxury of time. (In Spanish there is a nice word for the way I was travelling: *vacilando*. It can mean dithering, but also just hanging back, moseying at leisure.)

Soon I also discovered that apart from being cheaper, there is at least one advantage to the bus in this part of the country—it winds through some very attractive white hill towns that the train cannot. The first of these that both appeared and appealed was *Montilla*. A promotional sign in its main street read: "*Montilla's* scent. Discover it!" I thought again, "Well okay, but at least give me a reason rather than just urging me to do it."

Still though, to a certain degree, a little jewel like *Aguilar de la Frontera*—a town further on—could be enjoyed from a window seat. With its gorgeous Baroque-style clock tower and the pleasant old *casas señoriales* (nobles' houses) in its twisting main street, the traffic jam meant that I was close enough to sit and watch the town in its daily life. As is so often the case with leisurely travel, the beauty was in the unexpected details. My eyes fell on a cute little dark-haired girl, wearing a dress and sandals. She was patiently helping her father unload open boxes of striped orange frozen prawns, standing, then waiting, with her face blank and doll-like. A drama of purple lavender bushes in a nearby garden took my glance from her and then the moment was gone—the bus moved on.

Outside the town of *Monturque* I noticed the major road works that were abandoned, probably due to funding problems, and now there was a mid-morning haze hanging over the double-faced *Subbéticas* Mountains.

Next came *Lucena*, another white town up on a hill. In the Middle Ages it had been an independent Jewish republic within the Muslim caliphate of Córdoba, but persecution in the twelfth century meant that the town's Jews had to take refuge in Toledo, almost 400 kilometres away to the north. Today it was a sleepy looking place full of quiet furniture factories and retail outlets that were being ignored by the locals.

Sixty-five summers earlier another middle-aged Australian had been heading south to the coast (though unlike me, he had left from nearby Granada). Described in one of Truman Capote's articles for the *New Yorker* magazine as "wearing a soiled linen suit; he had tobacco-colored teeth, and his fingernails were broken and dirty." To Capote's surprise, this unnamed Aussie had been a ship's doctor and came in handy when the exterior of the train they were both travelling in was machine-gunned by some of the bandits who used to roam the area during that more anarchic time. The *bandidos* all disappeared as quickly as they had apparently arrived and no one had been shot, but the doctor bandaged an old man's head with one of Capote's spare shirts. It turned out that the old man had simply fallen off the back of a carriage where he had been stealing a free ride.

Like Capote's shirt, I was also of some use today. A couple of hours out of Granada, a voice behind me on the bus asked:

"Do you speak English?"

"Yes I do," I said and pivoted my head around to face a red-haired woman probably in her late forties, wearing a khaki singlet and shorts.

"Oh, what a relief! Just to hear someone who knows English. Nobody seems to speak it around here," she grumbled. Her name was Linda and she was Danish. She told me she was walking a stretch of the pilgrim's route, the *Camino de Santiago*, but yesterday decided to quit.

"I did forty kilometres the other day and there was nowhere to stop. The heat has been terrible and I was attacked by a pack of dogs. And where are we supposed to sleep? The schools are closed and that's where I stayed last time I walked the *camino* without any problems."

I asked her if it was for religious reasons that she was on the *camino*, an ancient trail that ends at the Cathedral in Santiago de Compostela, a 'holy city' where (amongst many other things) it is claimed that Jesus' foreskin is kept.

"Well, there's a lot of different reasons that I won't go into, but I'm trying to test myself, to see what I can stand. It's not easy, y'know," she explained. "I walked two hundred kilometres in nine days and that's carrying a fifteen kilo pack plus six kilos of water every day." Linda was apparently unaware that there is an easier way to do the Camino. One experienced pilgrim I read about said that you don't need to carry water because you come across piped water about every forty-five minutes and that it wasn't necessary to purify this water either.

"Actually, I try to be like a lion," Linda said, pointing at a tattoo of an animal on her upper arm. "They are special creatures. I worked with them for an hour in Namibia and I know their spirit."

We talked a little bit more about my life and hers—she had an Arab boyfriend and wanted to listen to some live flamenco music. She said it was interesting to her even though she'd never actually heard it before. While we were going down a sharp hill on the bus, she mentioned to me that she has MS—Multiple Sclerosis (an unpredictable, often disabling disease of the central nervous system that can even cause some people with severe forms of it to lose the ability to walk independently, or at all). I immediately expressed my admiration for her. Anyone going such distances on foot gets my applause, but someone with MS doing this day after day is nothing short of remarkable.

"Yeah, the MS slows me down and I get extra tired," Linda stated, with only a trace of despondency.

When she looked out the bus window I took a subtle, sideways look at her bare legs, expecting that I might see spindly, emaciated sticks. In fact, she had the muscular calves of an Olympic weightlifter. Later when I picked up her backpack out of the bottom of the bus in Málaga its heaviness confirmed that she genuinely was a kind of weightlifter.

Linda told me she felt bad about cutting short her time on the *camino* and flying back to Denmark and before we said goodbye she harnessed on her pack and put her two crutches under her arms. I too felt bad, mine a tug of empathy. I still wanted to help, but I don't think she even needed any.

Just like a travelling Juan Goytisolo in the late 1950s, Linda had "turned off toward Málaga in pursuit of greater comfort and pleasure." After what she'd done to herself on the *camino* I'm sure she deserved more than anyone's share of that. In a disturbing follow-up, the following spring a Chinese-American pilgrim named Denise Thiem disappeared on a more northern part of the *camino* at *Astorga*. After a massive police search she is still missing and a number of other women also reported being threatened in the same area. Two pilgrims were confirmed to have been tazered by men and this prompted the vague warning by the official *camino* website administrator, who announced:

"There has been some improper behavior reported towards women over the last few weeks on the stage between Astorga and Rabanal. These reports are sufficiently credible that we would like to make a general advisory that

pilgrims walking alone on this section of the Camino..., might want to walk in pairs or groups." The *camino* now had some real dangers. It was attracting people from all around the world but was not immune to tragedy and bad publicity.

⊗⊗⊗

SO, ANOTHER BUS STATION AND ANOTHER WAIT. I HAD NO interest in seeing the city of Málaga, save what I could spot from the bus window. Coming out of the station past the industrial port it was clear that it had at least one thing in common with a lot of the rest of the country: fresh-looking Roman ruins showed that Málaga too was digging itself up.

The view along the coast was as you would expect from a large Mediterranean seaside town in summer: high rise apartments until a mountain gets in the way then stretches of beaches full of sunbathers and the calm, blue-green sea at the shore. Predictable and pleasant but to me, as dull as a dentist's' convention.

That great romantic pastoralist Laurie Lee had also been underwhelmed by *Málaga* when he lived at *Almuñécar* on the coast nearby in the 1930s. Expecting "a kind of turreted stronghold, half Saracen, half Corsair-pirate," he instead saw "an untidy city on the banks of a dried-up river, facing a modern commercial harbour, the streets full of cafes and slummy bars and its finest building the post office."

Málaga has at least one point of interest that might have delayed me a while though. It has a long history of dealing with both the living and the dead of England, having been the site of the first Protestant cemetery on mainland Spain, the *Cementerio Inglés*. It opened (outside the old city walls) in December of 1831, putting an end to the practice whereby only Roman Catholics could be buried in consecrated ground in Spain. As a recent article in the Irish Times reported, "in *Málaga*, the custom was to treat the non-Catholic dead as heretics and to bury them upright on the seashore at night, leaving the bodies to the harsh mercies of the waves and animals."

I decided to bypass the cemetery. Instead I changed buses at the town of *Nerja*, where in the late 1950s an Australian radio celebrity named Shirley Deane had lived with her artist husband and young children until she was expelled by the Francoist authorities. They took exception to some of the contents of her book *Tomorrow is Mañana*. During the very same years on the other side of the mountains at *Lanjaron* at the craggy foot of the massive Sierra Nevada range, Juliette de Baïracli Levy, an English traveller, was writing her modestly-titled memoir *Spanish Mountain Life*.

In this innocent, lyrical book she details her personal struggle against a typhus fever plague, her education about herbal medicine from the gypsies of the area and how she gave birth to her second child—a baby girl who had to be suckled by a nanny goat. I could see that the town of *Nerja* had an inviting beach, but I was on my way to meet an expat Englishman from Shropshire named David Baird.

He met me at the mountain bus stop of his adopted hometown of *Frigiliana*.

"Hello, sport," he said, using the lingo that was popular in 1970s Australia. He'd lived there then in a remote northern mining town called Mount Isa. Small and very darkly tanned, David is a writer and former journalist. His beard and hair are almost completely grey and his bushy eyebrows nest above a pair of compassionate brown eyes. After we'd had a beer together we trudged uphill, slowly climbing through the narrow and roughly cobbled "steep stepping streets" of the town. They were not wide enough to drive a car in and I dragged my heavy suitcase with its hard plastic wheels behind me.

"That's the noise that usually wakes me up in summer," David said. "When I first moved here it was the sound of the mules clip-clopping along. Now, it's tourists like you," he joked.

His small house was high up and the back terrace overlooked the old part of town. The view curved down a handful of kilometres to an expanse of sea framed by the *Tejeda* Mountains; the horizon was ruled off by the bluest of skies. Ten metres below the house was a new open-air restaurant owned by some South Africans, David told me. Most of his neighbours were no longer Spanish and yesterday the town had lost another of its natives—an old man that David knew had just died. Today the funeral was to be held and David felt obliged to go.

"You'll probably be able to see it all from here," he said pointing across to the main hill, while we stood on the terrace. "The mourners are going to walk through the town, carrying the coffin as they go through the streets, and I'll join in at the back I suppose."

While David was gone I had a nosey poke around his empty house. Thea, his Dutch wife, was out too. It was like stepping back in time to my childhood of the 1970s. In one room that smelt of time—in other words, musty decades—there was a huge collection of cassette tapes and singles and LP records, including Ike and Tina Turner. Other shelves were filled with little plastic boxes of Kodak photo slides. On another I saw all nineteen volumes of an original set of that information dinosaur: the Encyclopedia Britannica. Just as touching to me was the fact that there were books jammed into (and on top of) every flat surface—proof that a good writer is a big reader and maybe a hoarder too.

In the almost windowless kitchen they had assembled a fine assortment of locally made ceramic plates and bowls hanging on the rough white walls. In the toilet down a set of narrow stairs I also noticed products from the middle of last century. One was called Zynkalf and was German, or possibly Dutch. Packaged in a tin with that particular shade of blue that you don't see in shops anymore, it was something almost from the pre-plastic era.

When David and Thea had first moved in at the start of the 1970s they were like pioneers. There was no electricity, no modern plumbing and the streets were unpaved. The house itself may well have originally been a barn. They had done what many dream to do: live simply, cheaply and without pretense. I admired that.

I also greatly admired David as a writer. To me, he is one of maybe a few dozen people who had made Spain what it was to today's English-speaking world population. His articles and books extolling the beauty of its scenery, the liveliness of its people and the romance of its history were all factors in drawing large numbers of British to visit. They spend money and, in more than a million cases, live here, especially along the southern coasts.

One of his works particularly grabbed me as well as inspired me. Titled *Between Two Fires*, it is the kind of nonfiction that can only be written by someone who has spent a significant amount of time living in the country. In this book David writes with a feel for the people and past events in their lives, but without the kind of party political allegiance that would turn it into a heavy polemic. Possibly because he was still considered to be a neutral outsider (even after having spent many years in the village) the townspeople trusted him enough to tell their stories.

Focusing entirely on the area around *Frigiliana*, David did immaculate research to write in compelling detail about the "people of the sierra"—those who took to the mountains, some to escape, some because they had little choice, and some because they expressed strong political opinions that led them to be tagged by Franco's cronies as "bandits."

One of the remarkable things about *Between Two Fires* is that the reader finds a Spain that is almost impossible to recognise in modern versions of this country. As David points out, at the start of the twentieth century the average person in Spain lived not much longer than thirty years. It was still very much a feudal land where even subsistence farming was only for the lucky ones. There were no public hospitals or public transport and mules and donkeys were the only way of getting any distance without walking in bare feet or simple dried-straw shoes.

It was a time of smugglers, travelling repairmen, mass illiteracy and child labour (often starting at six years of age). Progress took the form of a single 30-watt bulb being installed in a house, and after Franco's victory this part of the country also became a benighted land of evening curfews where anyone found in the streets after dark was automatically arrested.

It is unsurprising then that there was a significant level of support for the men who fought against authority in *Frigiliana*. While some townspeople were kidnapped for ransom by the rebels, it was the civil guard who were more hated (though both sides were feared, and for good reason.) If you helped the guerrillas, such as by providing them food or clothes, this was enough to get you thrown in prison, but to not help them at times meant to the outlaws that you were collaborating with their enemy and you could then be a target for recriminations. It is in this sense that ordinary people were caught "between two fires."

Apart from the clarity of David's writing and his even-handed approach (which is a relatively rare thing in the highly-politicised arena of Spanish history) at least half of the book is given over to those who were intimately involved in the events of the time. They are given page after page to simply tell their own versions. Their first-hand accounts are vivid, illuminating and often poignant.

I'd first met David when, along with a few other assorted writers, we'd been invited to visit the northern region of Asturias by the tourist board. He was sent off to the mountain hiking area of the *Picos de Europa* (literally, 'Peaks of Europe') and with a guide I was taken mainly around the mining villages and into the towns of Oviedo and Gijon. We'd got along very well and had dinner together after we'd come back from our allocated places.

Now a couple of years later on, we were in his local *Frigiliana* tapas bar swapping travel tales. David had once lived in Hong Kong and had also loved his time in Australia despite being posted in Mount Isa, an isolated, hellishly hot and remote town in Queensland where he was to work as a journalist.

"I was fresh off the boat and knew nothing about the politics of the place," David recalled. "The mining company ran everything in town and they sent this ruthless PR man named Asher Joel in from Sydney to take on a young Rupert Murdoch who was starting to expand his empire. Murdoch had made the mistake of backing a miners' strike and straight away kicked off a media war by starting up a rival newspaper. He guaranteed the union that his people's jobs were safe and that they would win the dirty war. Then, when readers turned their backs on the paper after they alleged that local schoolgirls were prostituting themselves, the money ran out. Murdoch just sacked all the staff and left."

Thea then filled me in on some of the high points of David's career. He was in fact a humble man and not given to bragging. They had been living together in *Frigiliana* when General Tejero's failed coup attempt against the newly elected Spanish parliament took place in early 1981. (Coincidentally, just a few hours earlier the bus I was on had passed through Torre del Mar, where Tejero has lived since his release in 1996; he served just over fifteen years in a military prison for his part in the 'mutiny.') David rushed to Madrid as soon as he heard about the gun-toting general with his two hundred soldiers and waited expectantly outside the parliament building with other nervous international journalists.

"*Tienes huevos?*" one of the local press asked him, meaning: Do you have the balls for this?

"They'd sealed off all of the streets so all we could do was sit pat until we knew exactly what was going on inside," David recalled. Together, we discussed the merits of King Juan Carlos' involvement. Thea believed, as many Spaniards did, that the relatively new and young monarch's decision to go against the coup and publicly support the democratic government was a big day in Spanish history. In fact, the long-time dictator Franco had groomed Juan Carlos to take over as an unelected head of the country, but when the king and the rest of the military sided against the plotters their fate was sealed.

Or at least this was the conventional view. It turned Juan Carlos into a kind of hero and ensured that he would stay on a Spanish throne as long as he liked. When he finally abdicated in favour of his son Felipe (six weeks before I left home) a royal decree passed by the council of ministers ensured that then-king

Juan Carlos and his queen Sofia would maintain their immunity from any future civil or criminal prosecutions.

ॐ

MORNING OPENED MY EYES AND AFTER BREAKFAST DAVID DROVE me higher up through rough winding roads into the mountains behind where he lived. At the edge of a forest I saw the same two-metre high wild fennel plants flourishing, just as they were near my faraway home: the same native fennel that Virgil's farmer *Simylus* had his baskets woven from, wherein he kept his round cheeses.

We stopped in a little restaurant with no customers and David chatted to the owners. On the walls were black and white photos of hunters, soldiers, children; this rustic eatery had been in the family for decades. He walked me through the little village. It was like *Frigiliana* had undoubtedly once been—quiet and seemingly almost unpopulated, with tiny narrow paths sloping up and down, flowers neatly decorating both sides, leading off to an old water well.

Then David drove us down to the seaside town of *Torrox* and we had some fish for lunch as we talked, looking over the beach. The next day David emailed me an article from the local press, as we'd been discussing the subject; a few hours before our lunch a thirty-seven-year-old woman (the director of the History Museum in the nearby town of *Nerja*) had been killed in her apartment in this same town. Her partner was the prime suspect. He reportedly had a history of abuse with a former girlfriend and had already been arrested after neighbours confirmed that they'd heard sounds of a violent struggle in the building.

This was a shock, but not completely unprecedented. Only three months before, one of the country's Catholic priests, a Father Pedro Ruiz, was reported to have said while conducting a first communion:

"Thirty years ago there was a lot more ignorance and perhaps a man (would come) home drunk and beat a woman, but not kill her like today.

Why? Because before there was a moral sense and today there is not. Before there were Christian principles and values. Even drunk, he knew that there was a fifth commandment that said thou shalt not kill."

So the twisted logic goes: it is moral to beat your woman, but only if you don't end her life doing it. This priest does his work in the inland province of Jaen and my next destination was Jaen city.

❧ 6 ❧

IN JAEN

The name of Jaen is derived from the Arabic word *khayyān* ('crossroads of caravans') but it's not immediately apparent as a junction of much at all. Trudging upwards, the old part of the city felt like it was at the top of a hill and when I got there I could see that it had actually been built into the side of an even taller mountain. Over the next handful of days, I was to find that Jaen is like that—it makes you work for your reward, but reward there is, at least for someone who doesn't mind a good walk.

But this morning the streets stank. They reeked of rubbish that had not been collected for two months due to a garbage collectors' strike. Bottles and bits of food lay on the ground soaking up the sun and in a few places there was the acrid pong of an uncleaned toilet. Unlike where I lived, dogs ran free here in the tilting narrow alleys. (I'd noticed that particular freedom in *Frigiliana* too.)

I tramped around the *callejuelas*—a beautiful Spanish word meaning side streets (but also trickery) and while I unsuccessfully looked for the old Jewish quarter, I heard a young man's voice singing *a cappella* flamenco from somewhere inside an apartment.

The area was poor—people were carrying shopping bags of what looked like their own domestic waste. A kind of graffiti battle underlined the feel of deprivation.

"*Moors go to your country*" one wall declared. On another: "*Reds out of Spain!*"

In a different public square, in bright red paint was a stenciled piece of street art saying: "*A little suggestion for you sons of bitches: Follow your leader!*" Under these words was a painted figure showing Hitler blowing his brains out with a pistol. In other spots, Nazi swastikas had been crudely crossed out in red.

A couple of streets away, though, there was redevelopment. For someone like me who enjoys "perving at old buildings" (as former Australian Prime Minister Paul Keating called his sightseeing in Europe) there were enticing ruins of something stony lying behind a long crude wall next to new flats that were being thrown up. At one shady street corner a simple yet lovely Romanesque fountain was still jetting out clear, cold water and its smooth rock edge showed that for hundreds of years bums had rested on it. I did the same on this already hot morning.

I was already thirsty again and my mind went back to that morning's breakfast. In a bar I had spotted a food custom I had not seen anywhere else in Spain. On each table and on the counter there were plastic bottles of fresh tomato liquid and another plastic bottle of olive oil—almost certainly extra virgin—and in each one there were a dozen whole cloves of garlic. Some high end restaurants in the province actually go to the extent of putting three types of top grade oil on the table, as a free garnish. Maybe this is unsurprising when you know that this relatively small part of the country produces more olive oil than any other Spanish region.

The people of Jaen are proud to point out that a lot of oil from Italy and Greece actually uses olives taken from their region. La Loma (just one of Jaen's ten municipalities) alone accounts for fifteen percent of the world's olive oil production.

Probably a more important fact is that ordinary olive oil is very cheap in this part of the world. Apart from in cooking, it has dozens of household uses, including to stop squeaking doors, and a nurse at my local medical centre advocates putting a few drops in your ear to prevent wax forming. Olive oil is also used by some Spaniards on their skin and hair to moisturise, while the practice of starting the day by drinking a cup of it before breakfast is still done, by older Iberians especially. In earlier times of history, the Romans used to use olive oil in the way we use soap today.

Over a generous glass of fresh orange juice in a different bar, I looked up to see that corrupt old Catalan ex-President Jordi Pujol on television again. This time he was shown going up some stairs at a park and tripping over—the literal fall and the metaphorical fall. In the local press I read that three thousand people from Jaen were getting ready to go to France for the month-and-a-half season of backbreaking grape picking. Here was an example of how Andalusians were still travelling to earn money, just as they had done historically. In the vineyards where I lived this kind of work was now almost entirely done by migrants from outside Spain.

In the same paper there was quite a bit of bad news: the city council was deep in debt and health unions were criticising the closure of hospital beds. In the nearby town of *Baeza* workers at a school of hospitality had not been paid for five months. This unsettled me because it reminded me of the kind of stories I'd read about in Russia years ago, and more recently in Greece. Wages unpaid on a wider scale across the country? That would be the start of the end, I thought, but it was possible I was being overly dramatic.

Of course all was not lost, in fact. Some of the populace were bent but they were not broken. In another town not far away a volunteer group was setting up 'cooking against the crisis'—a course to be run during the summer—and they were feeding twenty-three families during the difficult summer holiday months when school meals were not available for young people.

There were some unusual aspects to Jaen as a city, though. On one of the main streets there were tram lines and seats at the tram stops, but I hadn't seen any trams. Was it another strike? I asked some local men about it. Yes, it is a tram line, I was told, but a tram has never been on it. The line was approved and built but the town council stopped spending on it in 2011 after it had been used for a mere two weeks by the citizens whose taxes had paid for it.

Warming up, I took myself to the town's ancient Arab Baths hoping for a good soak, as anyone can do in the restored baths of both Seville and Barcelona, where luxury and comfort are abundant. Instead, I found that these baths were purely a museum. Entry to this lovely building was free, though, and a visitor walks down into the originally eleventh century musty subterranean digs of what was more recently a tannery, a poorhouse and then a women's hospice until 1970.

At the other end of the social scale and time scale, it had once also been a count's palace. In the cavernous, pillared 'warm-water bathing room' the *Almohad* Moorish arches echoed those of Córdoba's *mezquita* (as well as Granada's Alhambra) and star-shaped openings in the rounded stone ceiling let in shafts of natural light. It didn't take a lot of imagination to think of this place once resounding with the soft hisses of the Berber language snaking across the wet mosaic floor.

Spain loves its medals, awards and prizes (with their whiff of Freudian desire for parental-approval) but to me, the convincing, atmospheric restoration of these rooms fully merited the wider recognition they had been given across Europe. Today there were very few visitors and unlike, say, Granada's Alhambra palace, because of the small number of people there was more than enough peace and quiet to enjoy it.

Outside in the harsh sun a small but surprisingly well-labelled garden also felt authentic. Lemon and orange trees were set amongst a range of herbs and bushes, including a *cica* of Asian origin that created an intimacy to the space. Sitting alone in its shade was lovely; like living a few stolen moments from long ago

But it couldn't all be lovely, of course. Back inside the artificial light of the art space of the building there was a "naive art" exhibition. Room after room had been filled with the kind of flat and overly-colourful kiddy stuff that you can see on any parent's fridge door. This clashed with the solid integrity in an adjoining display, where examples of old wooden transport were being ignored by the few visitors inside. A gorgeously restored, hand-painted stage-coach sat next to a cart that looked like it had been made in the mid-1800s. It was actually dated from the 1940s and closely resembled the same thing that I saw being pulled by a horse the next day on a road just outside the city. A farmer wearing a flat cap was holding the reins.

So as was now almost a custom for me on this trip, at lunchtime I nosed around the town looking for somewhere to eat, using instinct instead of a guide book or website recommendation. At the *Peña Flamenca* (flamenco club/association) bar restaurant I saw that there was a cheap *menu del dia* (set menu) and a crowd of people drinking around the counter at the entrance. With a traveller's instinctive superstition, I took it to be a good sign that this group included two women who looked like my Australian grandmother and I was just as pleased to see that a couple of barmen were themselves drinking glasses of beer on the job.

Inside, though, no one was eating yet. There were several dishes of *cabrito* (baby goat) on offer but I plumped for a *gazpacho* that turned out to not even be chilled, some nicely cooked small sardines and a simple, decent salad of sliced tomato and lettuce. With a couple of glasses of white wine thrown in plus a substandard coffee and an overly polite, almost apologetic waiter, it represented that commonplace event for millions of working Spaniards: a midday meal (actually a few hours after midday) at a reasonable price; more than acceptable, but not in any way spectacular.

What made up for the unremarkable food was the general tone of this still virtually empty room. Black and white photos of performers who had once graced the now silent stage in the corner hung on the walls alongside portraits of other well-known dancers, singers and guitarists. But this was no Hard Rock Cafe. Live flamenco was a regular occurrence here, but when I asked, I was told there would be nothing until September—once again the usual summer slackness.

Listening to the recorded flamenco while I deboned my sardines and sipped the dry white wine, I was reminded yet again of how this kind of music has the ability to communicate complex emotions. With not only words but using specialised vocal techniques—sometimes even in a whisper—at its rawest it delivers a statement; no, that word is too intellectual, too clinical. Rather, it is a declaration sometimes akin to a human howl because it has a pre-industrial, unscientific essence. A flamenco voice, a true one filled with *duende,* is the call of a man or woman into the uncaring air—what Laurie Lee called "a naked wail of sand and desert." It implores someone to hear and is rich in desire for earthly justice.

An authentic flamenco voice will also wrench the heart, or if exactly the right note is peeled off, it has a different power. One hundred years before I was born, Matilda Betham-Edwards, when exposed to gypsy guitar in Granada, gushed that "you are ready to make love or war." Another century before that, Henry Swinburne said that Andalusian flamenco dancing "exceeds in wantonness all the dances I ever beheld. Such motions, such writhings of the body and positions of the limbs as no modest eye can look upon without a blush!"

I have had some very similar sensations. One night in Barcelona a buck-toothed young woman suddenly, and only for a few minutes, took charge of the microphone at a flamenco music students' performance that had been mainly mediocre up to that point. When she hit her first note it set fire to my groin in a single instant.

This time, sitting there at the Jaen restaurant table, my eyes filled with tears and I had to struggle to suppress letting out a sob. In ninety-five percent of my life I am no dewy-eyed romantic, but once again flamenco had seized me and shaken me up. The singer in the recording I was listening to seemed to be working himself up into a state of heightened emotion from a deep wish to communicate something from his subconscious. He was using so much more than the brain to summon up the sound he made.

Possibly, this is one of the same ways that a writer might attempt to put himself in a condition where the words flow, seemingly with no apparent thought. *On The Road* author Jack Kerouac believed that "the first word is the best word." He maintained that stream-of-consciousness prose was the closest to hitting the 'moment-idea of the instant' in the same way that jazz music was an improvisation that gives form to the spontaneous.

Back at the hotel for a late afternoon siesta (which in Spain is often not actually a little sleep) I saw half a dozen kids on the local TV station singing and dancing in a flamenco talent show. Most performed competently, but the powerful voice of one girl of about fifteen provoked kisses and long hugs from a male judge. The extraordinary confidence of some of the contestants was mixed with a precocious posturing. Oddly, one of the captions referred to 'money in the shadows.' It made me wonder if there were also other things in the shadows backstage.

☙❧

ONE WARM NIGHT JUST OUTSIDE THE CITY'S BUS STATION, IN A dark corner against a wall there were two people. A man was lying down on a large piece of cardboard box with his back to me and with him was a woman sitting up. I excused myself for disturbing them, told them I was a journalist and offered to pay three euros for a short chat with them. As I said this, the man woke up, bleary-eyed, and instinctively shifted his body between me and his partner. I repeated what I had said and he agreed to talk. I gave him three euro coins.

"Have you been staying here long?" I asked.

"Well, it is four months now," the man said. I noticed he was shirtless and the woman was toothless. Both were somewhere around fifty years old.

"Is your girlfriend okay? She looks a bit sick."

"She's fine. She shoots up sugar but I don't touch drugs or alcohol," he insisted. Talking almost to himself, he said some other things I didn't catch, partly because of his strong southern accent that tends to leave out pronouncing some sounds, especially the letter S. He repeatedly looked at his wife with a caring expression on his face.

"And do people treat you okay here?"

"Some people swear at us but we don't get bothered by the police," he stated.

"And why are you sleeping here?"

"That judge in Madrid ..." he began and looked away, gesticulating with a stiff arm in the direction of the national capital. "What a stupid decision! Now her nephew has the house. We're locked out and there's nowhere to go. The Red Cross is closed until September, what can we do?"

The man's voice was loud, animated and at times incoherent. It was as if the judge had amputated his happiness and it would never grow back. He put his hand on my shoulder, asking me if I understood. I lied that I did.

"How would you be in my position?" he demanded to know, though I took it as a rhetorical question.

He was just one of Spain's homeless. Some press reports estimated that every day there were almost another hundred more on average.

Now the man was ranting more. He drew his finger across his throat and I glimpsed an angry look in his eyes. I didn't know if it was because of me or not. I started to feel afraid because he was also still grasping my shoulder. Then his partner started to say something to explain or maybe calm him down, but I shook his hand and backed away, thanking them profusely for their time and wishing them good luck and good night.

Straight back to the hotel room; I washed my hands, feeling still shaken up by what might have been a threat. I looked in the mirror and picked two little black lice off my pathetic balding forehead.

ঙ্গত্ত

THE NEXT AFTERNOON I WAITED IN THE SQUARE OF THE CITY'S
massive main cathedral. The power of the sun meant that it was
virtually deserted and I enjoyed an open view across the pleasingly
understated geometric mosaics in front of it. Here I met a man
named Rafael Cámara Expósito, a spokesperson from *Tarbut
Sefarad*, Spain's largest Jewish heritage organisation. We talked in a
quiet cafe and I asked him about his background. Was he himself
a Jew?

"No, but my grandmother has the name of a *converso* (a Jew
who by force or choice converted to the Catholic religion). Her
name was Manuela Viedma Abolafia." Rafael wrote down on my
notepad a variety of spellings for her name since medieval times
and explained one of these is on the recently published official
government list of *conversos*.

"So I feel a connection to the Jewish people," he said. "I have
lived and worked all my life in Jaen and I know that the Jews
contributed a great deal to this town and Spain overall. Around ten
percent of today's population here has Hebraic origins so it's difficult to not have some kind of link with the Sephardic past."

"But what do you think is the average person's attitude towards
Jews? I have read some surveys which show that anti-Semitic
feeling is still very high."

Rafael frowned. "I can tell you for sure that there have been
negative opinions of Jewish people, but I believe that is changing.
The situation in Gaza and Palestine has not been helpful, though.
It has brought out some changes in the mentalities of a minority. If
this was an anti-Semitic country we would have seen public
protests against the establishment of the various memorials we
now have. As well, there would have been large-scale complaints
against the government's recent decision to allow those who can
prove that their ancestors were expelled all those centuries ago to
come and settle here."

Yes, maybe, I thought, but possibly it was a case of the populace not really knowing or having bothered to notice those changes. Just because he and I already knew about them didn't mean that they were common knowledge across the country.

After Rafael kindly insisted on paying for the drinks, we left the cafe, planning to walk together so he could show me some sights related to the Jewish history of the town. He pointed to the cathedral, asking me if I was also interested in its history. I said in a polite tone that I wasn't. Rafael seemed indifferent to my reply and proceeded to give me chapter and verse about this decadent monstrosity that has all the humility of Donald Trump.

Finally walking away down the lovely pedestrian walkway of Calle Maestra, we came to a vaulted niche set at the second floor level of an ordinary building. Behind the clear glass of a wooden frame I could see a cross with the crucified figure of Jesus and some small vases of flowers. Rafael explained that this was a Christ of the *Amparo*, the protector.

"There is a legend about this particular statue of Christ," he began. "In medieval times a procession was heading towards the cathedral when a single Jew stepped out of the crowd and tried to profane the Lord by pulling down the large cross that a man was carrying. Another man stopped him, but a fight broke out. The image of Christ appeared above them and on seeing this the Jew immediately dropped to his knees and converted to Catholicism."

Later, I read a slightly different account of this story, involving a local Castile official, Don Miguel Luca de Iranzo (himself widely known to be a convert), who was said to be leading the procession. This version of events maintains that it was a 'group of Jews,' not a lone individual, responsible for attacking the symbol of the cross and that it was Iranzo who "reacted by hitting out and many other Jews then fell on him (whereupon he) invoked the Lord and a blinding flash was projected onto the wall where the vaulted niche is located today, revealing an image of Christ."

There are many other similar stories across Spain that have put Jews in these kinds of roles. In a harbinger of the twentieth-century holocaust, in pre-1492 Jaen they were made to wear red or yellow circles on their clothes to identify them as 'the other.' What Rafael told me next gave me a more nuanced picture of how they were placed.

"Of course, the Jews were the property of the King," he said. "And this fact gave them a status where they were protected, to a degree. They were highly valued by the nobles for their skills and were useful to the business world as a significant part of it. In fact, *conversos* had a major role in opening the first banks of the time."

We walked on and in a different part of the old town arrived at a small open square called *Plaza de Huérfanos* (orphans) that was near where I had been exploring through rubbish and graffiti the other morning. In the middle of the space (which a generous person could call seven-sided) Rafael led me to an oversized replica of a *menorah*, the traditional votive Jewish candelabra with its seven candle holders. Dedicated to the *Diaspora*—those Jews spread across the world outside Israel—and referring to the Semitic 'bond with the town,' the memorial plaque accompanying it can be translated as saying "the footprints of those who walked together can never be erased."

As if to echo this notion, a wooden bridge had been reconstructed only a handful of metres away and Rafael invited me to walk over it, just as the Jews of the Middle Ages had done every day to cross over a small waterway that still trickled. This marked the main entrance to an edge of the ancient Jewish quarter here at Jaén's all-but-disappeared Baeza Gate. Unlike the cities of Barcelona or Girona or Toledo, here there were no tourist shops to take advantage of Semitic traveller groups.

As Rafael and I moved on, all the while he was stuffing me full of dates, facts and names. His ability to recall these details in such easy profusion impressed me. He had the passion and historical sense of a rabbi or an original Zealot, one of biblical Judea's sects and quite possibly his distant blood relatives. I changed the subject at one point, bringing up the garbage strike when we passed a pile of rubbish in a side street. "Do you think it looks like there's been a strike?" he wanted to know.

This was only the second question he'd asked me in the couple of hours we spent together. When I asked him if I could use his name in the book I was writing, he said, "Not if you're going to be critical of me." I assured him I wouldn't be unfair at all. As we said goodbye he asked me to pose with him for a photo for his Facebook page.

I left Rafael thinking to myself that it was astonishing how often in modern Spain (as well as Catalonia) you would keep bumping into Judaism, eight hundred years after it had been violently expelled from all the royal lands of the peninsula. As in much of the rest of Europe, it was sometimes hidden, but it was there nonetheless. Until very recently, Judaic culture and its remnants had been roundly ignored, and in many respects they were even still.

'PROVINCIAL.' THIS IS A WORD IN CASTILIAN SPANISH THAT HAS the same translation in English, but with some different connotations. It can suggest an uninteresting place, somewhere too comfortable and conservative, but also slightly backward and inward-looking: somewhere that lacks modern or cosmopolitan sophistication. The tainted word 'provincial' had been applied to Jaen by Antonio Muñoz Molina, as well as others in a number of conventional travel guides on Jaen—literally the provincial capital —and it had also been labelled as dull.

On my final night I was starting to agree with summations of the town as not a particularly desirable destination. In a 'frying' bar whose name translates into 'The Little Fishes,' after a free, sit-down *tapa* of bread topped with tasty *iberico* ham and roast red peppers, I ate a well-priced, well-cooked late dinner of squid (tails) and baby clams in garlic-parsley sauce with good local white wine.

A pretty decent meal, but in short, I was somewhat disappointed with Jaen. The service at dinner was atrociously slow ('SHIT SERVICE' I had written in my notebook) and as I sat waiting for the next course, I couldn't help but condemn the locals for being as unadventurous as they were apparently purported to be.

Here were middle-aged men, all in their checked, button-down short-sleeve shirts, and the younger men, every one of them dressed in plain or pastel-coloured polo shirts. These were the two de facto summer uniforms of the male European and I disliked them for their conventionality because they symbolised something else that I couldn't put my finger on at the time. Probably, my nerves had become naked and raw after weeks of travelling in the extreme heat, and this despite the fact that I am the closest human type to nature's reptiles: a sun-lover.

Now I thought of how tomorrow I would be in Antonio Muñoz Molina's original hometown of *Ubeda*, finally so close, and my hands busied themselves fidgeting in impatience. This creeping irritation made me question myself. What the hell was I doing? I was such a long way from home and there were no guarantees that I would find anything worthwhile or memorable the next day in a remote town I had never even set foot in.

I continued to look around the bar. It was apparent to me that the old Spanish habit of throwing your paper napkin directly onto the floor of the eatery had not died out here. What had also persisted was the general custom of eating out, especially in the summer months and on the weekend. The economic crisis had completely killed off spending by the poorest of the working class, but it looked to me like the rest of the country still had enough to go and have drinks and *tapas* until late into the night.

Sitting there near the busy kitchen, I had the thought: 'Yes, the smell of the freshest seafood being cooked is a uniting sensation—this is something virtually everyone has in common here.' A large majority of Spaniards have long considered themselves to be middle class (or at least in surveys declared it to be that way—a clearly false notion) but on a warm night like this it felt as if it could almost be true.

My legs were aching, but something made me walk for half an

hour up the street with the non-functioning tramline. To my surprise, it took me into a part of the city that, after several days, I had not yet seen. I'd left the newer part of the city near the bus and train stations and found myself in an area that was older and more attractive. It had covered portico arcades, fountains.

Next to a large cathedral, on two levels there were squares full of people eating and talking in the open air; table after table of the well-fed, well-heeled and well-waited on. Even the outdoor lighting was spot on and tastefully unobtrusive. There must have been a wedding or function on nearby because even the young people were formally dressed.

This was Spain at its absolute unaffected best: men, women and children of all ages socialising smoothly together in large groups— many obviously close-knit families—wines and water on the table, and all this without a hint of confrontation, challenge or disruption; Spain at its easiest, where it knew who it was because the question wasn't even asked. This crowd of cohesive diners had not been rocked by financial hardship, or at least they were not letting it show tonight in the warm air and the nicely comforting breeze.

I didn't want to leave this scene. It was purely and simply a setting of my dreams, *the great night of Europe*. My disappointment with Jaen had faded in minutes and I had become a convert. Something lovely caught my nostrils. It was the joyous and democratic, ozone-tinged aroma of frying fresh seafood again. For a moment, I wondered if the beggars (who looked like gypsies) moving through the tables—and were being completely disregarded—had smelt it too. Were their mouths full of water, as mine was?

But now I became self-conscious and realised that what I was doing must have seemed out of place. I was standing in a public place, leaning against a low wall looking, around intently, then scribbling in a blue notebook.

I was over-reacting, though; nobody noticed or cared. In Spain you can do almost anything if it doesn't badly disturb others. I watched friends meeting up, kissing on both cheeks, boyfriends, girlfriends and old friends. Here I was completely without any friends, it occurred to me somewhat pathetically. I had enjoyed observing the better off folk at their leisure. It had renewed my faith in what I was doing so far from home, and I decided to walk on back to where I was staying.

Back down in the lower part of town was an entirely different social event. Across from my hotel there was a celebration of 205 years of Ecuador's National Day. I had seen them when they started eight hours earlier in the afternoon: the kids playing in the sun and the adults all in the shade, but now the crowd had swelled and the music was louder too. It was just before midnight and children were still running around. I was just grateful they weren't playing that insipid, hopeless/hopeful, bleatingly bovine panpipe music that South America so often insists on.

❧ 7 ❧

IN ÚBEDA

The Andalusian town of *Úbeda* is on UNESCO's world heritage list, but who would know it?

In 2003 it was judged to have met their criteria related to its central area having "outstanding early examples of Renaissance civic architecture and urban planning in Spain in the early 16th century," but finding the town's tourist office on foot from the bus station took me the best part of an hour. And I had the advantage of being able to ask the locals for directions in Spanish, not English, which few would have understood here.

In Castilian Spanish there is a quaint phrase used by someone who is irritated, maybe at a business meeting or political gabfest: *"Irse por los cerros de Úbeda."* It means to wander around *Úbeda*'s hills and refers to a person who starts digressing and rambling either unconsciously or deliberately to avoid answering a question. The phrase has its origins from the twelfth century when King Fernando III was about to attack *Úbeda* and one of his captains disappeared just before the battle. He came back after the city had already been conquered, and, when asked where he had been, said that he had got lost in *Úbeda*'s hills.

I didn't get lost in its hills, but I had a hard time finding my destination—the final place I wanted to see before I turned and headed for home.

Every travel event has an endpoint. I should explain why mine was here. For years I had been touched by the acute empathy in the writing of a man who originally came from *Úbeda*, the novelist and journalist Antonio Muñoz Molina. I'd decided to see where he grew up to get a better sense of who he once was, even though I knew he now spent his working and married life in the big cities of New York and Madrid. I had the theory that a writer can grow *despite* his background and surroundings (or directly from them) and had the inclination to learn where this sensitive man had first found the intimate history around him that marks his later work as an adult.

Having turned up, I had no address for him, only harbouring a notion of possibly finding the part of the town where he had lived. Near the bus station, I asked a man where the tourist office was. His directions sent me down a street with plenty of traffic, but I soon learnt that there was no tourist office that way.

At that moment, I remembered the writer Fiona Pitt-Kethley's European travel maxim: never get advice about where landmarks are from *men*—they are too busy looking at young females to know where most things are. After twenty more minutes of asking a number of local women in shops for help I finally found it down a narrow one-way street. I did not see a single sign for the tourist office anywhere.

The lone woman working behind the desk handed me a map of the town and when I asked, told me that Muñoz Molina still visits often because he has friends and family in the town. She wrote down an address for where he used to live, only about one hundred metres outside the limit of the ancient city walls.

I asked her if she had read any of his books. "*Jinete Polaco,*" she said, 'The Polish Horseman,' one of his Spanish prize-winning novels, this one based on the 'immediate experience' of his life and those of his elders. Like most of Muñoz Molina's work, it has still not been translated into English.

Following the map, I ambled through the town. It was quiet. There were few people out and about on this hot early afternoon and I came to a small park that had a beautiful sweeping view of lines of olive trees lulling the eye across to softly rounded mountains and the widest of blue sky horizons.

Down some stone steps there was an abstract-style statue of a soldier without a gun and the figure of a woman cradling a baby. At the base of the statue were two stone books. A young Antonio would have seen this. Maybe he had been inspired by it.

Only a couple of minutes' walk further on, coming from an apartment I heard the sound of piano scales being played. This matched the genteel bourgeois feel of the area and, turning into the street I'd been told was once Muñoz Molina's, I noticed that just like the small town where I live, there was still the occasional housefront that has a metal ring where you can tether up your horse. A builder was working outside a house and I asked him where the old home of the author Muñoz Molina was, though I knew which number it was. To my surprise, he knew the family well and asked me if I wanted to meet them. I said that it would be very kind of him to introduce me and he took me directly to the other side of the street, knocking on the thick old wooden door of a narrow, white two-storey building.

A short woman of about sixty- five years of age opened the door. She had auburn coloured hair and was dressed in a floral apron—the unofficial uniform of the older Spanish housewife. "Yes, I am one of Antonio's relatives," she said, standing in the doorway, her arms folded. What did I want to know about him? I told her that I was from Australia and was an admirer of his writing, especially his book *Sepharad*. She corrected me on the pronunciation of the title and began to talk more openly.

"He lived in the house next door. My husband is Antonio's uncle. You know, I was like a second mother to him. He used to play here in our house all the time. He had to work in the fields because his father made him, but when he was older he got a job at the town hall in Granada. Antonio wanted to leave and he went to university in Jaen. He was thinking about writing—all these different kinds of ideas in his head," she smiled to herself, remembering a moment half a century ago. "One day when he was a little boy he held up a single raw chickpea and asked me, 'Tia Caterina, why is it like this?' He was curious about everything."

"Have you read any of his books?" I asked when she paused.

"Oh yes," she said. "*Jinete Polaco*, and you know, we are all in it!" she laughed. "Antonio has won so many prizes, but he always comes back. Just last week he was here for the *fiesta*."

I thanked her for her time and wished her well. Stepping back, I noticed a small yellow plaque up between the front door and the garage door of the house next to Aunt Caterina's. It said: "The writer Antonio Muñoz Molina lived here for part of his childhood. *Calle Chirinos*."

Covering the tiny balcony above, a plain white curtain had been hung, allowing air and light to get in while maintaining privacy. It was the same method used in thousands of simple homes across Iberia.

At the bottom of the street was another park—this one less orderly and lacking any statues. There were half full beer bottles left standing and clothes had been spread out to dry across the bushes and on the concrete. It had the abruptness of an end-of-town spot, and I could see a major ring road on the other side skirting the outside edge of *Úbeda*. This road was not marked on my map, but a street sign informed me it was named Avenue Muñoz Molina.

To the sounds of cicadas I walked back towards the main part of the town. I was relieved that the culmination of this trip had worked out unexpectedly well. I had also been moved by the author's aunt—the proud but not boastful way she spoke about him. And when I saw an old woman carrying plastic shopping bags in the street—yet another *abuela* that looked like my grandmother, who I last saw alive when I was only nine years old—my eyes filled with tears in this faraway place.

I stopped and stood still. My memory transported me to when

my grandmother (with her Semitic facial features), my 'nanny,' as we called her, would cuddle me and comfort me while wearing her padded dressing gown, just as I always picture her. My mother said it was because nanny was large and fleshy that I loved her embraces. But in truth, it was because she is in the marrow of what I am and also, like Goytisolo, because of what he called a childhood that was "missing maternal warmth."

It seemed to me that a young Antonio Muñoz Molina could not have lacked women's influence in his developing years. I pictured the slow afternoon weekend lunches of his childhood: a grandmother or even two nearby with other aunts and probably female cousins all buzzing around talking in a typically lively Spanish way. And this every Sunday, every festival day, every public holiday, every Easter, every Christmas.

Yes, it was clear to me now: the domestic world of General Franco's traditional, small-town Spanish woman. Babies and children at the very centre, the budding boy-writer there too, probably quiet and submissive, but sharp with curiosity and his seeing eye. Mother, relatives, affection, care, love and food. Always food.

This background told me exactly why his writing regularly shows a subtle understanding of women that is rare in a male—writer or otherwise. It also gave me reason to think again about some of his male characters: the henpecked husband, the regimented office worker or the suburban sexual-fantasiser.

In sleepy rural *Úbeda* all of them had their place and surely still do. They are the other side of the coin: the products of a conservative social order that can stultify, benumb and even smother. As his Aunt Caterina had told me about the extended family being placed in one of his novels, "We are all in there." She may well have meant the whole town.

But now I came to *Úbeda*'s largest open square. It had the generous medieval dimensions of a typical Italian *piazza* with rich geometric cobblestone patterns and tasteful fountains. Similar to the 'frying pan' town of *Écija* where I had been the week before, some of the narrower streets had canvas awnings stretched across them to create some crucial shade.

I walked downhill on *Calle Real*, a pedestrian-only 'royal' slope towards the town hall. I could imagine water coursing through this street in years gone by. As recently as the 1970s many of Spain's streets were still unpaved, but like the famous *Rambla* in Barcelona, which was originally an open sewer, these byways could fall prey to the seasons too.

Amusingly to me, I have taken some delight in telling stunned Catalan acquaintances that their beloved *Ramblas* (including those in Barcelona) have taken their name from the word 'ramla'— Arabic for a dry river bed. They were an urban feature that even took the eye of *The Ugly Duckling* author Hans Christian Andersen when he visited Málaga. He was inspired to write a poem about that city's "raging, wanton course" of flood when the market stalls would be swept away from what had been their home in the dried-up river.

As with the ancient waterway in Jaen's old Jewish Santa Cruz district being a geographical separator of tribes, I found the old synagogue just twenty metres to the left of that walking street in *Úbeda*. It is neither marked on the map as one of the designated fifty-two "places of interest" inside the walled medieval town (barely more than half a square kilometre wide) nor is it officially included as an "area of tourist interest." When I got there, though, I found it was busy enough to have to make a reservation for forty-five minutes later. There would be no English language used in the guided tour, which was the only option to enter the synagogue, now called the Synagogue of Water.

Stepping through the doorway, I was first taken with how different the building was when compared to a Catholic church. From its backstreet location the synagogue was somewhat hidden and certainly not a showpiece in a large square.

Inside it was also dark and, as with today, would have had little natural light coming in. Quickly too, I picked out some of the similarities Judaism has with Islam: the place of worship has separate entrances and seating for men and women, there were no decorations with animals or humans—abstract patterns being preferred, with a reliance on jeweled items for dramatic effect—and a painting of "the evil eye" had been placed on one wall in an attempt to ward off bad spirits.

The small group, of which I was the only individual member —the others all being in pairs—moved quietly into the main chamber, which had been fastidiously restored. We were told that the synagogue and attached rabbi's house were fully rebuilt in 2006, using original masonry where possible, after a local property developer started to excavate the site for new apartments. Slowly evidence was found of the medieval use of the area.

Our female guide told us a stark fact of history: all of Spain's 200,000 Jews were expelled from the country in 1492 after the royals Ferdinand and Isabella had decreed it. Those who survived this forced mass exodus—and thousands did not—fled to places like Turkey, North Africa, and across Europe and England, becoming known as the Sephardim, *Sefarad* being the Hebrew name for Spain.

We were told not to touch anything on display and shown an exquisite handmade fifteenth century original scroll of the Book of Esther. In a room off to the side it was pointed out that a probable Jewish-Catholic convert had once been employed there as part of the notoriously cruel Spanish Inquisition. The royal coat of arms that had apparently hung there may have served as a protection for the 'work' done there.

Down seven stairs—always the number seven, our guide said— we saw one of the seven underground wells that the site once had. It was dank and dim in this tiny stone-walled cell and the well (that still functioned from a natural spring) had been used long ago as a *mikveh,* a ritual purifying bath.

Before too long, the group was led out through the gift shop and I took the opportunity to have a look in the visitors' book. Flicking through the pages, the only English entry I could find was from a British woman complaining about the tour only being available in Spanish and the four euro entry charge.

For more than five centuries the Synagogue of Water had all but been washed away by the tide of history, but very recently, like Spain's wider Jewish heritage, it had begun to make something of a quiet comeback. The previous day Rafael in Jaen had questioned the authenticity of this synagogue. Today, I took his comment as motivated by that peculiar kind of parochial, neighbour-town petty rivalry that was rampant across the Mediterranean.

Mother Nature was no respecter of parochialism, though. On the other side of the *Cazorla* Mountains National Park east of *Úbeda*, the south and west of Alicante province was suffering from Spain's lowest rainfall—its worst drought in more than 150 years. Century-old almond trees had withered to death after no rain for almost eighteen months.

As a result of the kind of bureaucratic problem that is still all too common in Spain, the farms of the region had been classified into two groups, and only the irrigated land closer to the coast was able to use water from the reservoirs there.

Astonishingly, these reservoirs were still full. The driest (so-called *secano*) area inland was forced to rely on rainfall that was virtually non-existent. On top of all that, this summer more than thirty tons of dead fish were removed from the wetlands down on the coast. They had perished from rising salt levels leading to reduced oxygen in the water.

It was not only dying marine life and dead trees that were attracting attention in this region. A few weeks after my visit, a gravedigger named Clemente, working for the *Guardamar del Segura* town council, was suspended from his job. Along with one of his nephews, he had posed with a corpse they had dug up for a photo (and it too had been shown the light of day) but this time in the public eye. The snapshot was posted and widely shared on social media.

Felipe Aldeguer, an elected official from the town, reportedly commented that the incident was "unpleasant, miserable." The body had been dug up after having been buried for twenty-three years. He added that in his opinion Clemente "had not acted in bad faith."

It was in this same region that the prolific writer and traveller Eleanor Elsner (who was born in England's Newcastle-upon-Tyne, the same city as my father) lost herself wandering through the palm groves of Elche in the 1920s. She noted: "It is a very strange and attractive place, utterly unlike anything else in Europe." On one of her long walks she had heard a "typical eastern melody" that she thought was coming from the tops of the trees. It was an old Moorish date-pickers song and was being sung by the gatherers of the fruit sitting high up on the huge leaves as they did their work. After relishing a cold beer and some juicy mushrooms swimming in olive oil at a busy bar I took the bus out of *Úbeda*, passing slowly through the nearby medieval university Renaissance town of *Baeza*. I could immediately see some of the reasons why just over a decade ago it had been placed on UNESCO's list of World Heritage Sites. The classical lines of its large but somehow understated cathedral was exactly to my taste and the Moorish stone arch that still provides a way in and out has a style that also appeals to my sense of history's formal grandeurs.

Even here, though, they had the ubiquitous Chinese shop, the kind of place that you can seemingly find anywhere in Spain selling cheap clothes and thousands of household items. The contrast it made with the feeling of permanence and solidity that the old town gave was hard to ignore.

❧ 8 ❧

TO HOME

From my base in the town of Jaen, I took an early Sunday morning slow train to Madrid where I would once again change trains. This was the same train that Antonio Muñoz Molina would have routinely used in his university days in the 1970s.

In one of the stories in *Sepharad* he tells of the sadness and unfulfilled exotic lust that one of his characters experiences while waiting for this train. It has the ring of the author's own personal melancholy and the kind of gorgeously unnecessary minutiae that comes from real life recollection:

"A woman was leaning against the railing of the observation platform; I was instantly overwhelmed with desire, the innocent, frightened and fervent desire of a fourteen-year-old boy. I wanted her so badly my legs trembled, and the pressure in my chest made it difficult to breathe. I can still see her, although I don't know now whether what I remember is in fact a memory: a tall blond foreigner wearing a black skirt and a black blouse unbuttoned low. I looked at her windswept hair and the brightly painted toenails of her bare feet. A deep tan brought out the gleam of her blond hair and light eyes. She moved a knee forward, and thigh showed through the slit in her skirt. The train started off, and as I watched she moved away,

still leaning on the rail and watching the disappearing faces observe her from the platform of that remote station."

This was exactly the kind of stuff I relate to: trains, desire, strangers, childhood, sun-warmed olive skin, and casual encounters from a slight distance. Muñoz Molina reflects it all back to me and legitimises my own imagination and particular way of sucking up details of life-moments. His prose evokes memories equally as skillfully as Proust or James Joyce but in a softer, more intimate way, almost a romantic way. In fact, *memory* itself seems to be the central hub of his work.

As well as this, Muñoz Molina's novels and his non-fiction writing are routinely at odds with machismo habits and group culture. More than that, too, his main characters are often distinct individuals who reject the strutting and posturing of the business world.

Apart from George Orwell, in all my years of reading I have never found a writer who so accurately renders both my own world outlook and internal landscape as this man from Andalucía, born twelve years before me. His is a tender reverence for so many *ignored* bits of the physical world, especially the comfort of little things in our domestic lives.

And ignored, or overlooked, is also a good way to describe most of the literary world's attitude towards him, outside of his native land. Aside from winning the biennial Jerusalem Prize (given to writers whose works have dealt with themes of human freedom in society) the previous summer, Muñoz Molina has a very low profile and many of his books are yet to be translated into English. Many Catalans don't even know his name, and like so many of the parts of Spain I had just been through, the riches to be found in his writing have largely been for the eyes of the Spanish only.

Maybe that is a reason why he moved away to New York; a move that can bring a particular kind of clear sight about Spain that only living away from your native land can do. His journalism that I read over several years in the left-leaning national newspaper

El País consistently gave that impression. It had the quality of someone who was virtually stateless.

I felt that living away from Australia for so long had also given me the ability to be much more objective about the far-off continent where I had been born and grew into adulthood. I got the distinct feeling that we both possessed the eye of the outsider: not completely without prejudice, but certainly free from patriotic idiocy and therefore a great deal closer to the cold-blooded truth. For me, this is a rare thing in a human, as well as a writer.

For a few nights in bed before sleep, I had been neglecting my companion book by Goytisolo in favour of Florian Illies' *1913: The Year Before the Storm*. But like one of Muñoz Molina's shy young things, this morning I sheepishly returned to Barcelona's "self-banished Spaniard" and his iconoclastic words shepherded me through the land to the capital. Most of the way there, in front of me was a pious-looking middle-aged woman reading *Los Cerezos en Flor* ("Cherry Blossoms") by José Miguel Cejas; first-hand accounts of the arrival of Spain's insidious *Opus Dei* Catholic cult into Japan.

Moving along the rails, I was pleased by the sight of soft mist spread out across the base of the mountains and the self-repeating olive groves continued to insert themselves between each town.

At the wine-growing area of *Valdepeñas* a group of at least thirty teenagers, boys and girls, moved through the carriage bellowing out chanted songs, but there was nothing threatening about their behaviour. A few of them seemed to be drunk and a few smirks and muttered comments from several passengers were the only results of their commotion. As a mob, they jumped off the train when it stopped, hooting happily down the platform.

By coincidence, when I opened my book only a few minutes later in my seat I read Goytisolo's description of his part (as a child) in a religious procession:

"*One day, dressed in (fascist) blue shirts and red berets, we walked down from the top of Sarria to the centre of Barcelona...Under the fathers' energetic batons we shouted until we were hoarse,...thousands of arms raised, children's mouths opened, flags, music, emblems, a theatrical apotheosis."*

So here again was the Spanish love of noise and spectacle, the joy of the crowd, the comfort of symbols, and young people as taken with it all as adults are. Perhaps this is only rivalled by the Spanish love of breaking rules.

In Madrid's main train station I was *preguntita*-ed once again, just as I had been weeks earlier on my way through. While trying to check some details of my ticket at an information window, an old woman stepped right in front of me in the middle of my inquiry. She was even more roughly dressed than me and was particularly short. I realised she was pushing in and starting her own 'little question.'

"Wait," I said firmly.

"Shut up," she barked.

"You shut up and wait," I countered. That was the best I could do in Castilian Spanish. She continued to talk to the young man behind the counter so I simply talked over the top of her, trying to continue my business. He ignored me and dealt with the old woman instead. Stunned but resigned to the situation, I fumed in silence, *preguntita*-ed in Madrid for the second time this summer. My travels had been book-ended by queue-jumpers.

But it didn't really matter much anymore. The trip itself was all but over and soon after I took my seat on the fast train to Barcelona. As if to remind me how much the experience of this kind of transport was more like a modern plane flight, but on land —an impression I had been left with last time I'd been on an 'AVE'—all the passengers were handed earphones in a little plastic packet. Here was a clear signal that we were supposed to dose ourselves with screened entertainment.

The fact is that this 'AVE' from Madrid to Barcelona is the most economically successful of all these fast train lines, but it will reportedly take over a hundred years to pay for itself. So what? I thought. Why should public infrastructure have to make a profit?

Again, on one of the 'AVEs' I could see very little outside but this time it was not only because of the extreme speed of the train. It was worse. My assigned seat was next to a window that had a high, wide frame. I had a view of hard grey plastic and little else except for a screen on the ceiling playing a mediocre Spanish comedy movie.

Earphones in, the bearded young man sitting beside me alternated between reading a biography of Steve Jobs and being fixated on his mobile phone. There was to be no chance of conversation. It was all one big mood-killer, so I found my own way to pass the time. Like someone on a slow steam train a hundred years ago, I read a book: Goytisolo, wee-wee-wee all the way home.

✺

IT'S JULY 1998. MY MEMORY FINDS US IN A HOTEL ON A *VIA Laietana*, an arrow-straight main drag that runs up from Barcelona's port area parallel to the famous *Rambla*. When *Via Laietana* was created a century ago, old houses and businesses were bulldozed away. Now this road carries both traffic and tourists on foot looking for an alternative route through the Gothic quarter of the city. My then girlfriend Paula and I had stayed a few nights here on our first visit to the city and I had written in my diary:

'*3.30 in the morning. Strange dreams and even more macabre thoughts (maybe induced by the anti-malarial drug I had to take in Zanzibar) e.g., old people killing younger people for their stronger hearts to transplant. Is there a book idea in that? I think I'm having a heart attack. Ha! Ache more like it, from the regret produced by the fact that I will probably never live in this inspiring city. I love it already. So does Paula. Quality everywhere with enough grunge-grot real-life refuse of society and spent previous lives and works hanging in the air...That word 'civilise' and its variants come to mind...(Bigoted Australian politician) Pauline Hanson on page 8 of* Vanguardia, *today's paper here. A move to the ultra-right they said, in a country which has "peace in the cities and a level of life that the world has envied.*'

❧

SO EVEN BACK THEN BARCELONA WAS INSPIRING ME TO WRITE, with the germ of a book idea from tatters of dreams in the warm European night. Now, in a much nearer past, I'm in an elusive city I never thought I'd be able to live in, waiting for a train to take me back to the place where I do live. I'm sitting on a metal seat at Barcelona-Sants RENFE station and the train is coming from Manresa, a town up in the mountains that gets so cold in winter that the locals call it 'Man-Russia.'

With the crowd both listless and expectant on the sweltering underground platform, a mist of nostalgia settled over me, centering on why I had first come to Spain. To my consciousness, it was an unconnected bunch of influences that had brought me to this part of the planet. When I was about twenty-five years old and still living in Australia, I already had a liking for flamenco music and dance and had marveled at film footage of Granada's Moorish Alhambra palace but I remember thinking that there must be a whole lot more to this land.

As a kid, I'd had little direct contact with anything or anyone Spanish, but in primary school I did enjoy a friendship with a classmate whose mother was from Spain and had left Franco's dictatorship for a new life in Australia. She had married a flamboyant chef named Warren Barlin who was running his own restaurant in the capital Canberra's Manuka district. His food was a favourite of the politicians who worked nearby when national parliament was in session. My friend's name was Emilio and he had a younger brother named Antonio who was friends with my own younger brother, Joel. Emilio was a redhead with a fiery temper and this was of course put down to his "Spanish passion."

Fast forward more than thirty years later. In the winter cold, I am standing outside my mother's funeral in Canberra, and a small, pale woman with wavy brown hair and freckles on her cheeks approaches me and asks if I remember her. I apologise that I don't. It's not surprising because I haven't seen her since I was twelve years old. She is Adela Barlin, Emilio's mother, and she has come to my own mother's funeral after all these years because she says my mother was kind to her when she first moved to the country. I was touched and wondered if this was a usual practice for Spanish people, despite having lived in Spain for a long time.

Before that, I had already found out that there is a lot to like about Spain. After a month of travelling in fascinating but demanding Morocco, our first hours in the civilisation of the south of Spain had felt like "that first swallow of wine...after you've just crossed the desert." On the ferry across the Gibraltar Strait, in a striking moment I heard a woman's laugh for the first time in four weeks (apart from Paula's of course) and that realisation had shocked me as well as refreshed me.

Out of a relatively liberal North Africa, that night, in a small *bodega*/restaurant in Granada, we ate a first-time feast of cold white asparagus with mayonnaise followed by garlic soup, and I decided I was starting to be smitten with this country. I was then saddled with a wish to live in it.

🐱

BARCINO, AS THE ROMANS CALLED IT IN THE FIRST CENTURY before Christ, was a modern metropolis that over the years I had come to not just love, but know very well. Like many appealing big cities it is actually a collection of small *barrios* (neighbourhoods) and further out small towns that have been subsumed into Barcelona itself.

My teaching work took me to private offices and companies in many different parts of the inner and outer city. Wherever I went, though, my own private Barcelona was the Barcelona of a million women on its streets, beautiful local women of all ages and sizes: sources of my daily lust and fantasies never fulfilled or even attempted. It was also my continual history lesson with its grand old doors and its ornate balconies that you had to look up to really admire, and that looking up always made me feel like a tourist.

I had few good friends here (at least ones that lasted year on year) but the city was like a friend itself. It has parts to its personality that I am still finding: an inviting square here, a tree-lined one-way street there. As much as anything else I got off on the gritty side of the city's character.

There was *El Raval*, a rough immigrant area (behind the now-famous, tourist-choked *Boqueria* markets) with its prostitutes and pimps still openly drumming up trade just as they had done for so many decades. For the first few years, I loved the tiny narrow alleys of the Gothic quarter, but that started to feel too touristy, and I got my fresh kicks when I ventured further out of the old town, exploring the somewhat calmer residential areas like *Gracia* and *Eixample*.

One day recently, I finally decided to visit Barcelona's notorious *La Mina* district. I'd been told by a number of locals not to go there. It was dangerous, it was depressed and it was violent and full of drugs, several locals said to me. But like the author Paul Theroux, these warnings had the effect of making me want to go there and I could not ignore my intense curiosity. The notes that I made about this visit say:

Twenty-four minutes' wait for tram on this line. Tram past the hydro-electric plant and a waste treatment facility, simultaneously enchanting and frightening, through Besos, *in the strangely wide avenue people wearing tracksuits everywhere, groups of young men sitting playing cards, a group of pony-tailed gypsy young women in T-shirts, the mother wearing zebra stripes. Woman behind me: demented humming and another middle-aged woman sits next to me (for protection?) when the tram is almost empty. Worse than that—these are the poor immigrants (women in hijabs walking slowly and obese South Americans) who can't leave—to go back to what? Do they even have the money to? Most surfaces graffitied, rubbish uncollected, same run-down feel as the East Berlin-style ghetto/Lakes Estate (near Bletchley in England where I used to be a daily supply teacher at a high school that was smack in the middle of the highest teenage pregnancy rate in Western Europe.)*

So, I was bold enough to go there, but also coward enough to not get off the tram.

Yes, like the Jewish philosopher Walter Benjamin (who died tragically suicided a few hours north of Barcelona near the French border) I was often stimulated by urban life's darker side, but I personally also loved this city for its appealing little peculiarities, ironies and almost unknown but vivid histories.

Radical Barcelona: hometown of Ramon Mercader, Trotsky's icepick assassin with his dreams of a new world. Bloody Barcelona: the nineteenth-century killer-barber-cannibal-meat pie-cook who did his deeds with a trapdoor on the now heavily-graffitied *Pou de la Figuera* Street. Branded Barcelona: its main square *Plaza Catalunya*, where the Apple company megastore now sells pricey tech out of the building that was once the Communist party headquarters. Sleazy Barcelona's *'Barri Chino'* neighbourhood: stagescape for Goytisolo's (and countless others') pained or pleasured sexual discoveries.

Undeniably, though, it is Gaudi's architecture, the beach and the shops that are deservedly drawing tourists to the point where it is now the fifth most visited city in Europe (behind London, Paris, Rome and Berlin.) But for me it is so much more.

For one thing, it is where I have ended up working. As I finished writing this book, I worked in an IT job on the major through-road *Diagonal* Avenue with a window looking up the incline of the Via Augusta, the same originally Roman road that I live a few hundred metres away from and the same one that I noticed being unnoticed in Córdoba, more than eight hundred kilometres away. That kind of link with the history of two millennia ago, I also love. To be just another foot soldier in a long line of civilisation makes me feel humble and we all need that sometimes.

Heading for home, this train runs out through Barcelona's 'mean streets' that never seemed quite so mean to me. At *L'Hospitalet* I see cranes and huge sites being dug up: evidence of maybe some confidence finally coming back in the construction sector.

These new buildings are rising up right next to those who have gone before. Here's a cemetery's shelving system, the deceased placed one on top of the other with their tribute flowers, all open to see from the train window. Like so much else in Spain, the dead are not necessarily hidden away behind walls or fences but instead become a common feature of life, as it is experienced daily.

Very soon we stop at *Cornella* (also on the river and once prone to severe floods), another working class area. I feel the cheer of mixed memories: very early in the morning walking through the November cold of a rundown industrial landscape, a happiness of independence in this grim world, and being free from the drudge of secondary school teaching for the first time in a decade and a half. I picture the unemployment lines I'd see already forming outside the Social Security office near where the sewage smell comes up from the underground grates in the streets and recall that every Wednesday morning I would be here, just to teach English to the owner of a gasket factory.

In this area, my habitual RENFE train line follows the *Llobregat* River for a stretch. A small (unnamed) town somewhere on this river was the main setting for a subtle, engaging memoir titled *An Unknown Woman*.

Written by Lucia Graves (the daughter of English poet/novelist Robert Graves and translator of bestselling author Carlos Ruiz Zafón's *Shadow of the Wind*), amongst many other telling observations in this work, she recollects how in the Franco years it was commonplace for the well-off Spaniard to order books "by the metre" simply to fill up shelves: a habit that suggested that their content was wholly unimportant to the householder, and that books were for decoration rather than something to nourish the mind.

We make our way past Barcelona Football (i.e. soccer) Club's superb training ground at *Sant Feliu* and then to *Molins de Rei*, a town named after the King's Mills that once existed in this area. In the early twelfth century, mills were built here by order of the Aragon King Alfonso II (also called the Chaste or the Troubadour) a noted poet of his time and a close friend of King Richard the Lionheart.

I remember heading to work on a different day on this same train. I had read VS Naipaul's note about Flaubert's mill slaves being cruelly muzzled to stop them eating the flour they ground while dragging themselves around, pulling the wheel like beasts of burden in a never-ending circle.

I wondered what it was they milled here beside the river at a time when it must have had a more decent flow to it. Long ago in a different feudal era Catalan bread was made from crushed broad beans. Or maybe the king's flour was made from corn, in a food habit stolen from South America.

According to translator Peter Bush, "Catalonia's industrial revolution started in the late eighteenth century with the manufacturing of textiles, and this meant that where there were rivers in the countryside there might be power to drive the looms, so you find factories in rural areas." It seemed to me that *Molins de Rei* was an example of a once rural town that now felt like it was the last part of the wider Barcelona conurbation.

Also along this train line, through a valley that makes a natural transport corridor, on the sides of buildings hundreds of business names can be seen, and there are those that are odd and slightly comical to an English-speaker: Willi Betz; Fungilab; Uponor; SICK (Sensor Intelligence;) Robatech; Christher; Flippers International; Fagraf; Luk Fag; Praxair (slogan painted in green English words: "Making our planet more productive," while its huge smokestacks belch out grey-white cloud;); or Gonvarri (a traveller with a venereal disease?); then Consman; Topcon; Joyman; as well as the sinister, Nazi-sounding Gestamp and Werfen Group; Gutser; Rammer; and finally, Masachs (pronounced 'Ma sucks').

To complete this singular strangeness, beside *El Papiol* railway station you can laugh at the decrepit brothel with a red door (marked *infierno*—meaning hell) and a blue door (*paraiso*—for heaven.)

Just before the station at the town of *Martorell* with its smokestacks and behemoth backdrop of the jagged Montserrat rock-mountains, there is an opportunity. Between the tunnel and a thicket of bushes, a rider on this train has twenty seconds for a view up the *Llobregat* River across to a truly unique bridge. Named the Devil's Bridge either because locals refused to believe that a human could make it, or because it was where a mythological Lucifer could demand the soul of anyone passing, it was actually used for tolls.

A little stone door at the top of its span bears witness to this role, and a bold Roman triumphal arch at one end tells how the original bridge was covered by the more recent one in the year 1283. It's a structure that had to be rebuilt after it was destroyed in 1938 near the end of the Spanish Civil War, but much of the original stone was re-used to fully reconstruct it in the mid-1960s.

I pass this extraordinary bridge regularly on the way to and from Barcelona and always give it a second look and a series of thoughts. For many years, whenever I saw this Devil's Bridge I used to automatically think of a similar bridge, the *Stari Most* in Bosnia, and I would picture how it was famously filmed being blown up in the war there two decades earlier.

History's hand has a way of reminding us of our disastrous mistakes. I see these bridges as just two examples of how civil war, only fifty years apart in the same Europe, can destroy beauty and ingenuity.

Of course both bridges were rebuilt, and this tells us too how non-human victims of battle can be resurrected. In *Martorell* there were other post-war success stories too. The Chupa Chup, a rounded lollypop that found its way right across the planet, came to be manufactured just outside the town. The product's association with 1970s television cop Kojak and its wrapper design by none other than surrealist painter Salvador Dali, meant that by 1980 the company had already sold ten billion Chupa Chups, with ninety percent of sales actually being outside Spain.

After *Martorell* the heavy industry ends and the fields start to give way to vineyards in all directions, spread out between the surrounding hills and mountains.

❦

STARTING THIS FINAL DAY, I HAD THOUGHT ABOUT HOW (outside of *our own* home) in one particular sense, I felt more *at* home in the south and west of the country than where we live in rural Catalonia. Mainly a question of language: I speak better than passable Castilian Spanish, but a number of times I had felt the sting of people refusing to acknowledge me because I didn't speak Catalan well, while they fully embraced our young son who is fluent in this language (which is, incidentally, not classified as a dialect of Spanish).

On the other hand, insults and discrimination against Catalan speakers were increasing—including inflammatory public statements from senior representatives of the governing conservative *Partido Popular*—and it seemed, in response, some Catalan people were allowing themselves to be pushed by this ignorance into being a much more extreme version of themselves.

One young man I know named Josep summed up an attitude I had come across in many Catalan people—a view I heard repeated again and again. "I have no interest in Spain," he told me one day. "It has another language, another culture and another history from mine."

These were not the sentiments of some uneducated rural hick. Though he had grown up in small town Catalonia, Josep told me that he was given a university education through a scholarship funded by the European Union. He knew that the same EU had poured money into roads and other infrastructure during his life and said that people in his country wanted to continue in the 'first level' of Europe, even though an increasing number of his compatriots were getting fed up with the bureaucracy and the financial cost of being a member state.

Josep struck me as a highly articulate guy. His was not the

bleating voice of a mindless, bovine follower waving a flag. "Joey," as he liked to be called, was internationally-minded. He had even lived in West Africa and spoke some German. The great question for Catalonia is whether he represents a majority opinion. It is a great question that dominates public discussion and continues to preoccupy the mainstream media, but where the country will ultimately go is still not at all clear.

෪

ON THIS SUMMER ESCAPADE I HAD TRAVELLED SUCH DISTANCES and had plenty of my preconceived ideas about Spain well-confirmed. But some of my more pessimistic expectations were not met, and that delighted me.

Now I had witnessed a much wider Spain too, brimming deep with dazzling history. It was less tired and muted than my day-to-day working life in the semi-industrial areas of Barcelona had shown me.

Out of my usual orbit I had expected more horror, more clear evidence of the economic crisis than reality threw up. Apart from some parts of Barcelona, the poorer regions were not (at least visually) full of miserable people and the unemployed were not ganging together on street corners as they had done in London or New York during the Great Depression.

Even though it is certainly comparable in scope and breadth with the worldwide economic and social disaster of the 1930s, today's "crisis" in Spain was simply not as visible as I had thought it would be. It was there—undeniably—but most of its sharpest damage was hidden from view and the public scenes of desperate mass protest in ravaged Greece were almost never repeated in Spain.

In essence, what I learnt was that instead, the family unit was bearing the brunt of the nation's troubles. On average during the year, ninety-five home evictions were happening every day as mortgage costs became too much for these Spaniards.

As well, the private world was regularly exploding into male-on-female domestic violence. The stress of greater poverty had turned some of these struggling Spaniards inward with bloody and grotesque results.

This was something I hadn't counted on finding and it had dogged my steps in virtually every newspaper I read in every town I visited. It was also a theme that spontaneously occurred in the months after my travel. I would look up at the wall of my commuter train and see a poster about it.

One day while sitting waiting in a government office, I read the text of another poster. *"Ya no tengo miedo al sonido de sus llaves."* Here, a woman was being shown optimistically saying: "Now I don't fear the sound of his keys (in the door)."

Across the media stories of great tragedy ran again and again. Even my local newspaper reported cases of domestic violence with a regularity that was alarming, and I became convinced that the problem was even more massive than I had pictured it. One of my female Catalan acquaintances tried to tell me that it was almost entirely attributable to South American immigrant men. I knew this was a hollow statement.

Still, I had based this trip largely on places I had never visited before in Spain's interior, a core of the country so often neglected by foreign tourists. I could have written as well about the UNESCO World Heritage listed giant rock pinnacles of *Las Medulas* (similar in grandiosity to those in Greece's more well-known *Meteora* region) or I might happily have rabbited on about the oxtail stew or the gleaming steel Guggenheim museum in Bilbao.

Equally, I could have extolled the glories of Girona's outstandingly preserved ancient Jewish quarter or of *Peñiscola*: surely the most picturesque of all white hillside towns. On top of that I may have chosen to rave about a host of other spots: dramatic and taciturn Toledo—arguably Spain's most historic town; Catalonia's *Caldes de Montbui* with its Roman history and natural hot springs built with their early 1900s feel; the perfectly preserved medieval alleys of Besalu; the Quixotic windmills of *La Mancha*; *Logroño's* vast plazas; *Tudela's* ancient spires and porticoes, or rugged and windswept Moorish Cadiz being pounded by the Atlantic ocean: so much more genuine for the serious sea-goer than the usually tranquil Mediterranean.

All these Spanish gems I was lucky enough to also see for myself and to walk through on my own feet. But these were on other trips with my family, when I was not alone and free from distraction. Now I was back among the vineyards, its vines, its thronging of soft green leaves and its grapes—a landscape I always carried in my head.

The magnet of the journey had first pulled me away, but I had learned so much about Spain, Antonio Muñoz Molina and even myself. That wish to rediscover and discover anew had been satiated for the time being.

My question about whether a writer's origins affect his work had also been resolved. At least this was the case with this author from rural Andalucía and I knew directly from his family that his novels did not attempt to deny it. His childhood memories, his adolescence and his young adulthood echoed through his places, characters and plotlines. On my own pilgrimage, they even merged into what I had seen, heard and tasted.

And on top of realising plenty of new things from talking to Spanish locals and expats, I had been tested, both physically and mentally, on the rollercoaster ride that independent (largely adlib) travel genuinely is. As much as I enjoy hot weather, being on a bus for three or four hours every few days in the middle of a Spanish summer takes its toll on a middle-aged man with average fitness and two malfunctioning kidneys. Yes, I'd eaten well and generally slept well (after hours of walking almost every day) but there's nothing quite like your own bed, after all.

Stepping off the train, I was flushed full of excitement to be back again with Paula and our son Hugo. I knew I was home the second that I caught the taste of a familiar minerally aroma in the air.

ACKNOWLEDGEMENTS & THANKS

Certain short extracts of this book were first published in *Catalonia Today* magazine between the years 2014 and 2018 and are kindly reprinted with permission.

A thousand thanks for a thousand reasons to the following people:

John French, David and Thea Baird, Sue Sharp; Rafael Cámara Expósito; Hilde Higgins; Antoni Cardona; all the wonderful staff at the Bellvitge Hospital's Renal Unit; the Hetheringtons: Paula, Hugo, Ron, Joan, Matt and Joel ; Barbara Tipson; Sue and Howard Clarke; Matthew Tree; Ibrahim Sajid; Sue and Eric Willmot; Sally Bird; Claudia Calva; Janeen Jones; Cornelia Kraft, Pedro Duarte, Mike Estermann, Robbie Kavanagh, Jennifer Camacho, Barbara Leonard and of course the entire continent of Europe.